Whose Language? What Power?

A UNIVERSAL CONFLICT IN A SOUTH AFRICAN SETTING

Other books by Frank Smith include

The Genesis of Language (edited with George A. Miller, 1966)
Psycholinguistics and Reading (1973)
Comprehension and Learning: A Conceptual Framework (1975)
Writing and the Writer (1982)
Essays Into Literacy (1983)
Awakening to Literacy (edited with Hillel Goelman and Antoinette A. Oberg, 1984)
Reading Without Nonsense, 2nd edition (1985)
Insult to Intelligence (1986)
Joining the Literacy Club (1987)
Understanding Reading, 4th edition (1988)
To Think (1990)

Whose Language? What Power?

A UNIVERSAL CONFLICT IN A SOUTH AFRICAN SETTING

Frank Smith

Teachers College, Columbia University
New York and London

Published by Teachers College Press, 1234 Amsterdam Avenue, New York, N.Y. 10027

Extracts from C. Macdonald and E. Burroughs (1991). *Eager to talk and learn and think: Bilingual primary education in South Africa*. Cape Town: Maskew Miller Longman. Reproduced by permission of the publisher.

Extracts from S. Murray (1991). Developing language competencies of the student teacher. *ELTIC Reporter, 16*, 3–10. Reproduced by permission of the author.

Library of Congress Cataloging-in-Publication Data
Smith Frank, 1928–
    Whose language? What power? : a universal conflict in a South
African setting / Frank Smith.
        p.   cm.
    Includes bibliographical references and index.
    ISBN 0-8077-3282-6. — ISBN 0-8077-3281-8 (pbk.)
    1. English language—South Africa—Study and teaching—African
speakers. 2. Language and languages—Political aspects—South
Africa. 3. English teachers—Training of—South Africa.
4. Language and culture—South Africa. I. Title.
PE1130.A2S65 1993
428'.007'068—dc20   93-19616

Printed on acid-free paper
Manufactured in the United States of America
99 98 97 96 95 94 93   8 7 6 5 4 3 2 1

Dedication

To the 1992 Wits AELS Honours students
who shared their schools, their homes, and their hopes with me
and to all other teachers and students of the future South Africa
this book is dedicated

Contents

Prologue *1*

1   The Walls 7

2   Week Zero 23

3   Shadows 29

4   Week One 39

5   Soweto 50

6   Week Two 59

7   Contrasts 71

8   Week Three 80

9   Possibilities 90

10   Week Four 97

11   Signs of Hope 105

12   Week Five 114

13   Preparation 125

14   Week Six 131

15   Alternatives 149

16   Week Seven 154

17   Aftermath 170

References *173*
Index *175*
About the Author *177*

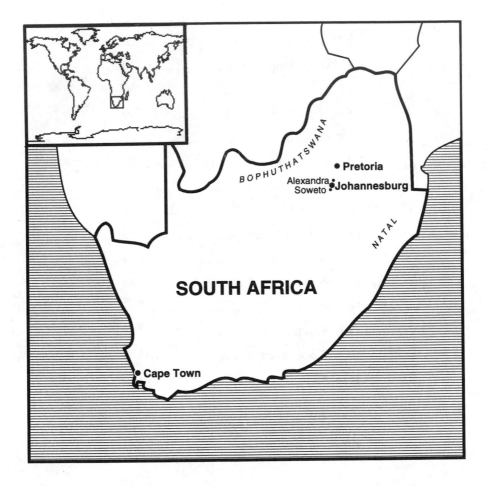

Whose Language? What Power?

A UNIVERSAL CONFLICT IN A SOUTH AFRICAN SETTING

Prologue

You taught me language, and my profit on't
Is I know how to curse. The red plague rid you
For learning me your language.

The Tempest, I.2

The term *empowerment* is frequently heard in contemporary educational contexts across the world, especially in relation to language and literacy. There is a widespread belief that political and economic conditions in entire societies would be improved if only individuals could "become more literate," "spell more correctly," or "speak better English."

South Africa is a case in point. There is currently massive concern with teaching English—or "better English"—to black students to help them rise from the subjugation of colonialism and apartheid. There is a prevailing assumption that fluency in English will enable large numbers of black students to succeed in the educational system, in university, and in the professional and political worlds. I went to South Africa to participate in what I believed was a genuine effort to bootstrap black South Africans into a "language of power." I had been persuaded that apartheid was ended, that significant reforms were under way, and that overseas contributions to help restore a shattered educational system would be welcomed. Black students would be taught English and "taught to think" so that they could take their part in the economic and political development of the country.

But it was sharply demonstrated to me that the development of language and thought could not proceed without concessions of power—and that emphasis on English language competence could maintain the disempowerment of the people it was supposed to assist. A focus on English in education could hold back educational and social advancement. Empowerment does not come with language; rather, language reflects power.

Other effects of language were brought home to me in South Africa. Statements of attitude, however strongly put and sincerely meant, do not necessarily betoken behaviour, and authoritative words (like the "fact" that apartheid has ended) do not necessarily reflect the actual state of affairs. The power of language may lie less in providing access to wealth and control or even to information than in enabling individuals to delude themselves as well as others. The greatest obstacle I encountered in the country—which will no

1

doubt reassert itself when this book is read by people involved in its issues—
was *rationalisation*, perhaps the most dangerous power that language
affords.

THIS BOOK IS MULTILAYERED. At its core is an event that might not appear
particularly noteworthy in many parts of the world: a seven-week seminar in
which a group of graduate students who possessed years of multiracial teaching experience explored together what they thought might be an appropriate
Honours course for themselves and for others like them on education and the
English language. The students struggled with such traditional educational
issues as the "best way" to teach a second language and to teach reading and
writing, the relationships between first- and second-language learning, and
the relationships between language and thinking. And they struggled to see a
way of overcoming the abysmal educational deprivation of most black African
students from primary school to (for a very few) graduate school. It all
seemed simple and straightforward enough, but it was not simple or straightforward at all. The seminar was entangled in a complicated mesh of past and
current events.

The seminar took place as part of the program of a newly established academic department. Uncertainties and tensions in the department and in the
seminar compounded each other. It was not only the students who were
striving to adjust to new possibilities and challenges in unpredictable and
emotional circumstances. The staff were as well, and their vision was not necessarily the same as the students'. Black students could look forward to a
potential increase in their authority, but white staff faced almost certain
diminution of theirs.

The university had its own compelling problems. It was struggling to
cope with a collapse in its financial resources as the South African economy
fell apart under the pressure of international sanctions and boycotts. As an
elite "white" English language institution, the university claimed a proud
record of asserted principle by admitting thousands of black students during
the days of formal apartheid. But it was now failing many of those same students, both generally and literally. Black students claimed they received a discriminatory, inferior, and paternalistic education from an institution that
turned away many black applicants because of arbitrary elitist "standards" and
then for the same reason rejected disproportionately large numbers of those
it did admit, though many were the hardworking successes and best hopes of
the schools and communities from which they came.

All of this took place in a violently divided and economically stagnant
nation trapped in the web of its own history. Among whites, there was a lack
of resolution or vision about the future—except among supremacist extremists. There was doubt and disagreement about the form the "new" multira-

cial South Africa should take, and there was reluctance on the part of many to give up more power and privileges than they had to. Many "liberal" white South Africans wanted to "bring the blacks up to our level"; for them, equality rarely meant equalization. Among blacks, in every way substantially worse off than whites, there was continual bloodshed and unrest, which sometimes directly affected seminar participants. There was seemingly mindless violence of blacks upon blacks, often attributed to provocations and instigation by whites, some of whom threatened retaliatory violence of their own against blacks and against moderate whites.

And everywhere there was anger, guilt, resentment, impatience, mistrust, fear, and suspicion. On the campus, memories were still raw of massive student demonstrations and of massive police responses with guns, gas, hoses, batons, whips, dogs, and vehicles indiscriminately used; of repressive regulations about what could and could not be taught, with informers in classrooms and staff rooms; and of deaths, detentions, deportations, and disappearances of students and academics. Writers had been prohibited to write and teachers to teach, speech had to be monitored, and many newspapers and journals were closed down. Such experiences left an ugly, poisoned environment for anyone to breathe and try to learn in.

Yet, nothing about the situation was unique. This must be stressed, though many South Africans might want to disagree. Similarly intense political, social, and educational dilemmas can be found all over the world. I would not have prepared this book if I thought it had relevance only to South Africa. I also do not want to suggest that I thought some South Africans as a group were particularly virtuous or that others as a group were particularly ignorant or malign. Those whom I met were all painfully human.

THIS BOOK IS NOT INTENDED to be an autobiographical record of my own feelings and experiences. I am sensitive to the temptation to rationalisation that I discussed a few paragraphs ago. But I cannot efface the part I played in the events I relate. I also do not want to focus undue attention on the individual students and staff who were involved in the events, although reference to them will be unavoidable. It is *situations* and relationships that I wish to uncover. My concern, as a teacher and researcher, is with education, with language and thinking, and with learning and teaching. These are the matters I want to concentrate upon. But all of these matters involve people and the particular settings in which events transpire, and I could not have produced this book as a dispassionate academic report even had I wanted to.

My approach is, as far as I can make it, "objective" or at least reportorial, based on extensive notes that became objects of mistrust among some of the people I worked with. I want to be impartial. But the first step in impartiality must be to acknowledge the central role I played in some of the events described. I was acting as chairperson of the department in which the events took place. I was responsible for the manner in which the Honours seminar was conducted. And I was told I was responsible for the disruption it undoubtedly caused the academic staff who had invited me to join them and for the disaster that some of them told me was the seminar's only outcome.

However, I do not want this book to be a defence of the role I played or an apology. If I could report on the events without reference to my part in them, I would do so. The experience left me bruised and disoriented, with new uncertainties about language, learning, and education. If I wanted to develop the argument that good intentions do not necessarily produce desired outcomes, I would not need to look beyond my own experience.

The book necessarily reflects my own beliefs and values and my own reconstruction of situations and dialogues. Other participants in the events would almost certainly give different accounts of them. My notes were never compared with those of anyone else. Nor have I shown a prepublication draft of this book to any of the people who appear in its pages; that would begin debates and "negotiations" which could delay the book forever. I was frequently criticised by my colleagues for perceptions and observations recounted in this book, and my colleagues often regarded my suggestions as unworkable if not wrong. At best, my contributions were accepted as "thought provoking," which is probably the way I responded to points of view that conflicted with my own. This is a story of complexities, and my aim is to uncover them, not to argue about them. I may be critical, but I have tried not to be condemnatory. Power, language, and education always depend on circumstances and personalities. Nothing is ever as simple as we would like it to be or often expect it to be.

THIS BOOK MAY NOT SEEM TO FALL into any easily recognizable category, so I should perhaps add a word about the genre into which it might be placed. This is not a didactic book (I am not trying to teach anything), nor is it an inquiry (there are no conclusions and recommendations). The book is not an academic monograph (there are no lengthy footnotes, the references are minimal, and other people's "work" is inadequately cited), nor is it a political tract, a sociological survey, or a programme for educational reform.

I would prefer to think of the book as a contribution to the discipline of applied English language studies with which the students in the Honours seminar—and the departmental staff—were so deeply concerned. The book is a study—in the sense of a detailed description of a particular situation or series of events—concerning the nature and consequences of English language use in one segment of a vast international educational system.

The book focuses on a group of people endeavouring collaboratively to achieve a goal of interest and significance, using mainly their own words, with a sketched-in background of the setting in which they live and work. As such, I see the book not as an end in itself but as part of a broad picture, much of which remains to be drawn, which can be the basis of reflection and action, following a growing tradition of ethnographic studies in comparative education.

AS EVERYONE REFERRED TO IN THIS BOOK is a real person, my first inclination was to use real names. But I could not identify the students, though they deserve acknowledgement and I am indebted to them all. Some students specifically asked not to be named in anything I wrote. In a nation of discrimination, they feared the consequences if employers or colleagues—or teachers—were able to associate them with particular expressions of opinion. Others did not make this request, but I can see that they might have the same concerns. And I cannot identify some and not others. On the other hand, the students were distinctive *individuals* in their interactions with me and with each other. I cannot ignore their personalities and treat them as a group or as nonentities. So, I have, with reluctance and apologies, given them pseudonyms. The students, themselves, will know who they are, and I leave it to them to decide whether they want to reveal their identities outside the group.

I could not do the same for my academic colleagues. There were fewer of them, and even with disguised names it would be too easy for them to be widely identified, especially if gender were indicated. And in any case, I cannot do the staff justice in these pages; their roles are painted with a broad brush although they are all complex individuals. I have the highest respect for some of the people I may appear to be most critical of—and who may have been most critical of me. All of them in their own ways—and some passionately—were trying to help black students move into a richer future and to make recompense for the past. I do not want this book to be personally about my colleagues any more than I want it to be personally about me. The book is not *about* individuals; it is about power, language, and education.

Finally, my use of words. Everything in South Africa literally reduces to black and white. Constant focus on colour might be called the South African disease. One white teacher who worked closely and committedly with black children and adults told me, "I still think of them as them and us. I can't help it. It is what apartheid has done." In my conventionally broad-minded way from my sheltered vantage point in Canada, I do not like to think of people in terms of colour and certainly do not like to identify them in writing in such a way. But one cannot adopt lofty positions in South Africa. The distinction is inescapable in discussions of the social and economic confrontations in the country, which are specifically based on colour.

I have considered alternative terms. The words *African* and *European* are rarely used to distinguish blacks and whites within South Africa. Europeans are people who usually live *in* Europe, and Africans may live anywhere in the entire continent. The Afrikaner descendants of early Dutch settlers, who speak a greatly modified South African version of the Dutch language known as Afrikaans, sometimes claim to have established themselves as a white African tribe. Blacks and whites refer to themselves and to each other as *South Africans*. Terms like *native* and *indigenous* are imprecise and often contaminated semantically. Euphemisms such as *tribal* and *traditional,* occasionally used in South Africa, are also imprecise and inappropriate as well. Scarcely any traditional tribal life is left in the country.

A common qualifier in South Africa connotes the distinction exactly, because it is a bureaucratic category based wholly on colour. It is the initials D-E-T, which stand for the Department of Education and Training, the national authority dealing exclusively with schools attended by black students only. But constant talk of *DET schools* and *DET students* obscures the broader racial issues in South Africa.

I considered using the term *unenfranchised,* which is also bureaucratically defined. Black people, by virtue of colour alone, have no vote in South Africa, though they constitute 75 per cent of the population (compared with 14 per cent whites) and are totally subject to its laws and regulations, some designed exclusively for them. But the word is rarely employed in South Africa in the way I would use it—as a descriptive term for individuals—and continual references to the unenfranchised would be cryptic as well as oblique.

When it comes to the point, I must use the terms *black* and *white,* which few South Africans, black or white, would hesitate to use. Skin colour is an ineradicable emblem that everyone carries, is categorized by, and profits or suffers from. It is a reminder that we are all prisoners of history.

Chapter 1
_____

The Walls

*A*partheid *is behind us. Barriers are crumbling. South Africa is rejoining the rest of the world. Any contribution to the reconstruction of the educational system will be welcomed. This is a wonderful time to be here. . . .* The invitations to spend a year at the University of the Witwatersrand were beguiling. Friends in Britain told me that South Africa had "opened up" like Eastern Europe and that it was now almost a duty to work with colleagues formerly isolated. No one tried to mislead me, but disillusionment came quickly.

The Johannesburg airport is like international airports anywhere, and the freeways are like freeways anywhere—until the clusters of shanties by the roadside are pointed out, improbable preludes to a modern city and its suburbs. But something oppressive about the atmosphere may strike the visitor. Perhaps it is the altitude and the thin and dusty air; the sprawling conurbation is a mile above sea level and has long, dry climatic doldrums. It could be the lack of coastline or river to draw the gaze or the absence of mountains to raise the eyes, for this is South Africa's high veld, the high plain. The tallest objects are downtown office blocks, and beyond them squat ziggurat dumps of gold tailings, reminders of why Johannesburg exists in the first place and why it attracted so many speculators, adventurers, and masses of exploited, unenfranchised workers.

In the suburbs, the visitor may detect the first sour scents of segregation and suspicion. Tree-lined streets may be full of fine houses and well-kept gardens, but most are hidden behind substantial walls—not decorative boundary walls but functional ramparts often eight feet high or more—so that it is impossible to see in or to see out. The walls may be ornamented with elegant columns and dentils, but they are probably topped with rows of spikes, broken bottles, or coiled razor-sharp wire. "Immediate armed response" warnings are posted conspicuously beside house numbers, and excitable dogs strain at locked gates when anyone approaches, producing a rolling barrage of barking if the visitor walks down the street. To show that the sidewalks are not for walking, the residents routinely park cars on them, forcing any pedestrians to step into the street. The only people to be met on foot—with rare exceptions in "bohemian" areas—are black maids and gardeners who work behind the walls at salaries equivalent to about five U.S. dollars a day. They sit or lounge under the trees chatting, as if they were back in some bucolic rural setting. They are surprised if the visitor greets them, and they may respond "Good morning, Madam; good morning, Master," with broad smiles.

Downtown Johannesburg is a busy western city on weekdays, especially in the financial quarter (though the big stores and theatres have begun to move to suburban malls). On weekends, the city streets are abandoned to blacks, who have made Johannesburg a bustling *African* city. Stalls line sidewalks; families have their hair cut under roadside parasols; women carry shopping on their heads and infants on their backs; and streets are filled with noise, colour, and abundant activity. Fleets of minibuses, organized by local entrepreneurs and known as "black taxis," bring genial human cargoes in from the townships and pack them and their purchases in even more tightly for the ride home again. Meanwhile, the weekday commuters stay home beside the pool behind the walls in the suburbs or take family drives out beyond the townships to the country's many fine animal reserves. White South Africans care greatly for the birds and animals that used to roam free across the countryside and allocate huge areas of prime land to the survivors.

Apartheid is over. The employers of the maids and gardeners often say they just couldn't wait for it to end. They only continue to employ their black servants because it provides necessary employment, and they may strain to get their bemused maids to call them by their first names. They sometimes pay the fees for their servants' children to struggle at white schools, and they encourage their own children to share the swimming pool.

They are sensitive about the difficult times they've been going through in South Africa, living in the eye of the world's censure, intellectually and politically isolated, their standard of living precipitously declining under the fetters of international sanctions. They deplore the violence in the townships and wish blacks were more ready educationally to take a part in the government of the country. They do not need outsiders to suggest how the situation might be improved; they can solve their own problems. They are coming out of a long period of colonialism and discrimination, with which they do not feel they should now be associated. The visitor is encouraged to deplore the horrors of apartheid and to enjoy its residual benefits. The visitor is welcome to join the people who live behind the walls.

I ARRIVED IN SOUTH AFRICA during the long antipodean Christmas-time summer vacation, and my new colleagues welcomed me at a traditional *braai* (barbecue) beside the pool, where I learned a little more about the realities of education in South Africa.

Seventeen different government departments control the country's education in a manic profusion of bureaucracies. Beneath an all-encompassing Department of National Education, white schools are administered by the four provincial governments. People of Asian origin (all called *Indian*) and people of mixed ethnic origin (all called *coloured*) have national school systems with separate administrative departments. Schools for black students (outside the ten artificial and internationally unrecognized black "homelands," each of which has its own system) are centrally administered by a monolithic State Department of Education and Training, known everywhere by its initials as the D-E-T. DET schools have historically received much less financial support than white schools, as little as 10 per cent per capita during the most rigorous days of official apartheid. The situation has "improved greatly" in recent years, with per capita funding of black students in DET schools now up to 25 per cent of the funding level for students in white schools. Over five times as much was spent on textbooks for each white student than for each black student in 1989, and in 1990 the teacher/student ratio in DET schools was 1 to 41 compared with 1 to 17 in white schools in the province of Transvaal, where Johannesburg is located. (These and other educational statistics are taken from annual surveys published by the South African Institute of Race Relations, Pretoria.)

Apartheid officially ended in February 1990, but the segregation of education remains. With extremely rare exceptions, only black students and black teachers are found in DET schools, and only white teachers are found in white schools. A few black children have been selectively admitted to white schools. Most of these favoured students have difficulty working at the same level as their white classmates and living in their culture. Black students' handicaps are widely attributed to inadequate skills in the English language and in thinking. A phrase often used to account for the discrepancies is that the black population has no "culture of learning."

There are also black universities and white universities and colleges of education for training black teachers and colleges of education for training whites. White students do not attend black institutions, which have the reputation among the whites of being "bush colleges." Some black students— "the best"—are admitted to white universities. There, my new colleagues told me, a distressing number soon run into problems of academic competence, attributed again to deficiencies in English language skills and thinking skills.

The University of the Witwatersrand, familiarly known as Wits (pronounced *Vits*) boasts a proud record of commitment to nonracial education and opposition to apartheid, reaffirmed annually at convocation ceremonies.

Currently, the student enrolment includes just over 25 per cent of black students, most of whom immediately encounter great academic difficulty. Various means have been tried to help these students meet Wits standards: Students may attend a pre-university school and participate in "academic support" programmes focusing on English language skills (reading, writing, speaking, and listening) and on study skills (such as note taking and précis writing), as well as sometimes receiving specific subject area tutoring. They may also take a special course in English as a Second Language (ESL), with an opportunity to obtain academic credit while working on English language and study skills.

The ESL course was an inherited responsibility of the new Department of Applied English Language Studies, whose first chairperson I had been invited to be. The department was vaunted as the only one of its kind in South Africa, a distinction somewhat attenuated by the fact that no one was sure what English language studies it should apply itself to. It had been established with the help of a substantial grant from an insurance company which might be expected to donate even more if acceptable proposals were submitted. What the insurance company anticipated as a return for its philanthropy was also not clear, though everyone spoke of improving education in South Africa.

The emphasis of the new department's programme and original staff was on teaching "practical" skills of English to black undergraduate students. This is what student and staff committees in the rest of the university felt was most important and looked for in the ESL course. Five of the seven founding members of the new department's staff had previously constituted a "communications studies unit" attached to the Department of Applied Linguistics and teaching the ESL course with a heavy linguistics emphasis. The other two staff members of the new department were seconded from the English department, where their main concern had been teacher education. Now their joint responsibilities were to be expanded into an entire degree programme somehow focusing on the English language and South African education. One of the seven was black, one was male, all were experienced teachers of English in South Africa, and all had done advanced study in ESL at institutions in Britain or the United States. Six of the seven were working on their doctorates or were expected to do so. There was one other overseas newcomer to the department, an associate professor who had also studied ESL teaching in Britain.

The seven original staff had been through a great deal together and were a cohesive and conscientious group dedicated to their teaching and their country, grossly overworked, and seriously underpaid. I had been invited to join them from the other side of the world to provide "leadership"—a term I mistrust, especially when it is written into organizational structures. In South

Africa, I could never discover what it meant. I had little opportunity to find out.

Two months after my warm welcome, I was ready to leave in impotent despair, and I did so three months later in an atmosphere of mutual frustration and disappointment. The account of what happened in those months is not really a story about me—which is the reason I can now conclude the most autobiographical part of this book—but about the seventeen graduate students, including six black teachers, whom I attempted to empower through language.

What happened to those seventeen students in the course of seven unaccustomed weeks of independent inquiry and thought will be related, largely in their own words, in the even-numbered chapters that follow. In the other chapters, I try to sketch the backgrounds to the student deliberations: political, social, educational, and theoretical. I would like to introduce the seventeen as soon as possible, but there is more to be said about the mood of the country and the educational problems that it faced.

FOR MANY SOUTH AFRICANS, both black and white, the beginning of 1992 was regarded as one of the best times to be in the country, a halcyon season of relief and hope. The National (Afrikaner) Party government of President F. W. de Klerk had formally announced the end of the apartheid "experiment" after forty years of official discrimination, repression, and fear. And after years of isolation, the country was basking in the warmth of international approval, with the imminent prospect of a reversal of the economic slide that sanctions had brought about. Many whites and blacks looked forward to an end of racial tension as they moved to a political accommodation on the future of the country: the "new" multiracial South Africa that would take the place of white rule. Blacks in general seemed forgiving and optimistic that the country was moving peacefully into a new era of black emancipation and self-determination.

The largest South African political party, the African National Congress (ANC), had been officially recognized and declared itself ready to work collaboratively with a white government toward orderly change. Its president, Nelson Mandela, released after twenty-seven years' imprisonment, appeared sagacious and conciliatory; he even appeared to have established a congenial personal relationship with President de Klerk. Scarcely a day passed without pictures on television and in the newspapers of the two leaders shaking hands or with their arms around each other in the business capitals of the world. Many South Africans, black and white, were saying how surprising it was to hear a black speaking to a white so confidently, assertively, and *equally*. The nation waited, proudly expectant, as its athletes prepared to reenter the international world of sport. They would demonstrate that South Africa's strength and spirit had not been broken during its years of being shunned and denounced internationally.

On the outskirts of Johannesburg, the opening meetings of Codesa—the Convention for a Democratic South Africa—were held in the spotlight of great international interest and publicity. The Codesa discussions were generally referred to by white South Africans as negotiations. They seemed to feel they were *bargaining* with blacks, who really would not push for untrammelled majority rule. The whites expected "compromise," though what unenfranchised blacks could compromise about was not obvious. Nevertheless, many whites thought they could "do a deal" so that their way of life would be preserved.

The worst seemed to be over. There was still violence and bloodshed—against a few white settlers in rural areas and among innumerable blacks in the urban townships—but these were regarded as local outbreaks, unpleasant but not nationally significant. Despite belligerent pronouncements by both black and white extremists, the country as a whole looked forward to peace and increased prosperity. Whites knew that change was inevitable, but they felt it could be kept under control. Everyone would be "reasonable."

The times were regarded as transitional, so few significant alterations were made to the social structure and no dramatic new policies were announced. These were all "details" to be hammered out by the working groups at the Codesa commission sessions. Substantive policy statements were felt to be inappropriate until there was agreement about the form the new South Africa was to take. Few people seemed to notice that behind all the words, very little was actually changing. South Africa was optimistic, and so was the new Department of Applied English Language Studies at Wits. The students and staff with whom I was to work seemed universally buoyant.

ORGANIZATIONAL MATTERS HAD TO BE ADDRESSED in advance of the arrival of students, and the broad, green, central campus was almost a vacuum, randomly intersected by molecules of preoccupied staff, bored security personnel, or administrators in low gear. The university, established less than a hundred years ago, grew out of the South African School of Mines, and the names and substance of its great buildings reflected the colonial and industrial history of the country. But like that history, the fabric of the university now looked meagre and threadbare. The libraries were housed in substantial buildings but had thin collections and were poorly staffed. Departments appeared neglected. Furniture was dilapidated, windows cracked, paint flaked, and shutters seized up. Money was short, and government priorities were elsewhere.

On the treed fringe of the grass-sloped campus, looking down on a huge, sparkling, open-air swimming pool, a relic of more prosperous days, stood the three-storey brick-faced Social Sciences building, sombrely accented with black-painted wood. Here, the new Department of Applied English Language Studies had been allocated a top corner set of offices, comfortably nestled among the Departments of Psychology, Linguistics, and Speech Pathology and an inexplicable campus width away from the Department of Education, where its primary interests were routinely addressed. The dark corridors of the building were lined with black doors with multiple locks topped by welded bars to discourage intruders from penetrating skylights hardly large enough to get vintage typewriters or the occasional computer through. But security was a constant anxiety. The staff were reluctant to set up a departmental library, even with donated materials, because "books only get stolen." A computer laboratory for students was regarded as out of the question.

The main concern in the pre-session departmental staff meetings was to review the courses that would begin as soon as the students arrived. Theoretical issues were occasionally raised, but the focus was always on the improvement of English language skills of black students.

The sole first-year undergraduate course, foundation stone of the new department, was ESL (the full title of English as a Second Language was never used), with an enrolment of over 200. Students with no particular interest in education, linguistics, or applied English language studies might come from across the university to take the ESL course. Often, they were required to do so by their home departments or by admission committees, simply in the hope of improving their English. In fact, registrants who scored well in matriculation English examinations found themselves excluded; ESL was not to be regarded as an easy option for students competent in English. The course was essentially for black South African students, although occasionally other students whose English might need some polishing—from central Europe or Asia, for example—were admitted.

Many dilemmas were associated with this course, which in various formats had a long history and reflected many of the university's basic problems. The fundamental aim was to improve the "basic English language skills" of black students. But the university did not regard itself as a "skills" institution; that kind of teaching was more appropriate for high schools or technical colleges. Its courses were expected to be "academic," open to all qualified students. Some professors felt that students not competent in the language of instruction should be elsewhere. Certainly, white students with similar English capability would not be tolerated. But many faculty members thought the university had a duty—or at least a desperate necessity—to bring the black students it admitted up to "white standards." There was always a conflict—within the university, within the department, and within individuals—about the relative balance of the "skills" and "academic" components in the ESL course.

The problem was bedeviled by the question of evaluation. Marking was central to the university's approach to teaching and was rarely questioned, but the allocation of final grades was highly problematic. It was argued that black students would not willingly participate in courses that carried no reward. It was obviously unreasonable to expect them to devote a quarter of their first year to a demanding course that carried no "credit" and that did not "count." But should black students receive credit for a course that would be trivial for white students? And should the majority of black students be permitted to pass the course, in which case the marking would have to be generous, contrary to the usual inclinations of many of the staff, or should the marking be tough, in which case many of the students would fail? (Black students were rarely discussed in any context without the affectively loaded words "succeed" and "fail" coming up.)

These issues of content and grading reflected dilemmas in other courses that black students and white students shared competitively. Either the instructors had to have double standards, black students had to be prepared to have vast amounts of extra work and tutoring with no guarantee of success, or everyone had to be resigned to white students in general getting the top marks and black students getting the lowest ones.

The solution reached for the ESL course had been to keep it essentially black only but to give full academic credit for it. Final grades were typically low but were fine-tuned so that not too many of the students failed. The course had been painfully revised the previous year to reestablish an emphasis on "skills"—at the insistence of university committees narrowly concerned with the written English of black students—as an adjunct to "academic support" programmes also designed to boost black English language competence and study habits. The course teachers, on the other hand, had tended to emphasize more theoretical aspects of language, partly under pressure from their former home in the Linguistics Department to maintain "academic standards."

What distinguished the course for a visitor was the massive amount of required reading, note taking, assignments, and marking associated with every session of the course, a burden for both staff and students that involved over 200 pages of photocopying annually for each student, all of it subject to examination at mid-session and at the end of the year. This was a course in which everyone was constantly busy. I was not directly involved in planning or teaching the course, and there will be little said about it in the following pages. But the tensions involved in the course and the issues associated with it permeated everything else in the department.

The only second-year course was a new one, about to be presented for the first time. It had been planned in "blocks" to suit the experience and interests of the half-dozen staff members who would teach it, and it included blocks on phonetics, phonology and morphology, syntax, semantics and pragmatics, language and learning, standard language and language variety, and language and social control. It was designed for students who would eventually become teachers of English or who would teach in the English language. Many of these students would be white students with a background of "academic" first-year courses in English or linguistics, but many others would be black students who had graduated from the "skills"-oriented ESL course.

A major dilemma for this course was once more to ensure that it was not beyond the academic capacity of black students—at least not to the extent that disproportionate numbers of them failed—but also that it was not elementary or boring for white students. The course had been planned by the group before my arrival, in consultation with people from other departments and elsewhere. I was to teach the language and learning unit of this course.

A third-year course was being prepared for introduction in the following year to complete the undergraduate program, making a major in Applied English Language Studies possible and confirming the status of the department. The same topics as those in the second-year course would be taught at the "English specialist" level (there was little alternative, as these topics were all considered essential for English language teaching in South Africa). There were lengthy discussions on how topics might be made "more advanced" yet still leave something to be taught at the Honours level. The Honours course itself—the focus of this book—was to come up in great detail and with high drama at a subsequent meeting.

There were also plans in our small but busy department to admit students for "untaught" dissertation-only master's and doctoral degrees. A nonacademic concern also awaited serious attention: This was the prospect of further substantial support from the insurance company that had underwritten the establishment of the department in the first place. The additional funds would be used to establish a Centre for Applied English Language Studies, although what such a centre might do and the form it might take had scarcely been contemplated, much less debated, under the pressure of getting the department on its feet. But the matter could not be neglected much longer if the financial opportunity were to be capitalized upon.

OBVIOUS SOCIAL AND PEDAGOGICAL PROBLEMS were associated with all the department's courses—problems that are general across South African universities and, indeed, in many parts of the world. Many of these were problems that might usefully be addressed by a Department of Applied English Language Studies with the requisite will and resources. But they were problems saturated by historic and political considerations. Some were so delicate in South Africa that the department regarded it as improper even to talk about them.

There were the practical problems of teaching anything to students diag-
nosed as deficient in English, the university's sole language of instruction,
and in learning and thinking skills (though the nature of these ineptitudes
was not clearly specified). There were the organizational problems of teaching black students and white students together, when those with a background in white schools almost invariably did better than those with a background in black schools (which often meant little or no educational
background at all). The pervasive university emphasis on written examinations and assignments exacerbated these first two problems.

There was the problem that efforts to teach "better English" to mature
students did not work conspicuously well. There was little demonstrable success for any of the university's efforts. There were many anecdotal claims for
the efficacy of "academic support" programmes in English for black students,
but nothing that might be called evidence.

The typical departmental reaction to all of these issues was a sincere determination to do better what they were doing already but not to do anything
different. Much time and effort had been dedicated to getting where they
were now, and there was little time or inclination left for "experimenting"
with alternatives.

There was the fundamental question—rarely asked in the university—of
why English should be made the sole or primary language of instruction in
South African schools at all. Should this movement be encouraged or even
acquiesced to? Why should the language be made compulsory in schools as
opposed to simply being made available? The universal use of English would
not be achieved without cost. To make English a compulsory subject in
schools would make it yet another subject that many black South Africans
would fail. To make it the required language of instruction would increase
the failure rate of black students in many subjects. These were contentious
and emotional issues widely studied by committees and commissions elsewhere. The department's preference was to sanitize these issues by making
them academic topics for detached treatment in courses rather than active
issues requiring deliberation and decision.

There was the same response to the question of which English should be
taught. Which pronunciations, which spellings, which idioms, and which syn-
tactic structures should be regarded as acceptable or appropriate in the new
South Africa? Should students be required to demonstrate some kind of competence in "standard English" as spoken and written in Britain (or in the
United States or in Australia) or was there an "international English" that
might be used? The department opted generally for an "academic English,"
defined no more precisely than as the language in which articles were generally published in academic journals. But why should the department determine such matters? Should language styles be mandated at any level? Why

shouldn't the standard English of South Africa—if there were to be such a language—be the Black English that seemed to be developing? Why should the way most black Africans spoke and wrote English be categorized as wrong? These were not matters to be considered as a basis for action, although some of the issues might again be treated neutrally as course content.

Then there was the question of *when* English should be introduced if it was to be employed on a wide scale in schools. Would many black children ever learn to read and write if expected to do so in a language they understood only imperfectly (and which their teachers probably understood only imperfectly as well)? One of the persisting consequences of apartheid was that many black parents had learned to despise their own language. Less than fifty years ago, many were still being forcibly educated in their mother tongue (using missionary grammars) so they would not get ideas above their station; thus, the indigenous languages became associated with slavery and oppression. An effort to impose Afrikaans as a medium of instruction ended with the bloody Soweto riots of 1976. English was identified as the prestige language, and many parents today demand it. The situation in many black schools—as it was then painted to me—was of total immersion in total incomprehension. But these were all "political" issues not to be confronted by the department, whose job was to teach about the English language the way a Department of Russian Studies might teach about Russian.

There was a sweeping concern with the "mechanics" of speech and writing, with theoretical analyses of pronunciation and grammar, and with spelling. Obviously, many students would always do badly if they were evaluated in ways that focused on these superficial aspects of language. The staff were quick to assert that they knew these "finer points" were not intrinsically significant and should not be considered from an elitist point of view. Nevertheless, they were important in the academic and commercial worlds and always demanded pedagogical vigilance. The staff conspicuously corrected the spelling errors in one another's handouts at departmental meetings.

Evaluation created intense problems. Being required to *produce* English was difficult for many black students, however well they might understand what they heard and read, yet they were *tested* in English in every subject. Writing is difficult enough for most students, especially under conditions of stress, but was particularly so for black students with limited experience in expressing themselves in writing and in the language they were required to write in. And they were expected to do all this—to understand the questions (perhaps by mentally translating them into another language), think of appropriate responses (and possibly translate them back from another language), and put the responses into an alien writing system—in exactly the same amount of time given students far more experienced in the English language. Giving all students the same amount of time was considered only fair.

Reducing the demands of evaluation was not to be contemplated. "Knowing how well students were doing" and marking every piece of work that was done were the basis of learning. They were the way standards were maintained.

There was the question of *how* to teach English. There was not much doubt in the department. Lecture analytically on the correct forms, give lots of examples and appropriate readings, require students to write sentences and paragraphs as often as possible, and provide swift feedback on every error that was made. It was acknowledged that there were alternative points of view—that massive correction might not produce desired outcomes, that it might only teach students what they could not do, and that independent reading had been shown to have an important role in language learning—but the department was not ready to try them. It would not be fair on the students. They were particularly aware of the work of Krashen (1985) on the importance of "comprehensible input"—of automatic second-language learning from what makes sense, provided there is no affective interference. But the response to this and to all other alternative points of view was to make them "content"—to try to squeeze them into already crowded courses, which did not otherwise change. Among favoured justifications for this obdurate position was the "fact" that black students were accustomed to rigidly structured "transmission" styles of teaching and indeed preferred them as they did not have the habit of thinking for themselves.

There was extensive awareness that all students needed more experience with independent thinking. The solution was to include sections on thinking in the courses. "Thinking" was often conflated with "study habits," like note taking and paragraph writing. The staff were aware that language and power were related; their concern was with empowerment. Their solution was to include sections on language and social control in the courses, encouraging students to look out for hidden messages in advertising and for examples of sexism and racism in language generally—considered not as a reflection of prejudice and intolerance but as the cause of prejudice and intolerance.

There was even a problem with the name of the ESL course. English as a Second Language was usually quite inappropriate. Most black students were already multilingual, learning two or three vernacular languages in their early years while communicating in their communities and with their peers. Most of the students also spoke and understood some form of English, learned in a variety of ways—at school, in occasional jobs, from acquaintances, and even occasionally from reading. Domestic servants usually knew some English; their employers could not be expected to speak African tongues. Many black students also had some competence in Afrikaans, in many ways the most prominent of the two official languages of the country but ineradicably linked with apartheid and repression. Often, the only monolinguals in university classrooms were white instructors.

There appeared to be an underlying faith that language instruction would bring about social change with minimal social disruption. The staff of the new department were not without their own differences of opinion, especially about the content of the courses, and many compromises had been made in order to accommodate everyone's interests and points of view. But the staff were convinced of the value of English. The result was a great deal of cohesion among the original group and a tendency to hold on to what they had with such effort achieved and to close ranks against alternative possibilities, which were sometimes frankly regarded as obstacles.

The characteristic has its own name in South Africa. It is called forming a *laager*, from the days in the first half of the nineteenth century when early settlers and their descendants, the Afrikaans-speaking *boers* (farmers) set out on epic *voortreks* (expeditionary marches) to establish their own independent homelands, escape colonial control, and retain slaves. When their efforts to stake out territory were opposed or they were threatened with the prospect of giving ground, they made a circle of their wagons—a *laager* in Dutch—and withdrew inside. Unable to advance and determined not to retreat, they closed in on themselves to fight grimly for what they had achieved.

A WEEK LATER, WE WERE LOCKED INTO DISCUSSION of an appropriate Honours programme for the Department of Applied English Language Studies. The course to be given at this level had been previously taught by the same staff as an Honours course in applied linguistics, and they had already decided that it should be taught and evaluated in much the same way.

The previous year's syllabus had comprised three blocks of syntax, two of phonology, two of second-language acquisition, one of first-language acquisition, one of discourse analysis, one of sociolinguistics, and two of language policy and planning. Each block was the equivalent of one afternoon period of about two hours every week for a "quarter" of seven weeks. Part-time students, who were the majority, took a total of twelve blocks a year, three each week of each of four quarters, over two years. Full-time students completed in one year.

The current year's offering was expected also to include the topic of language and power. Additional periods for full-time students and for second-year part-time students were fully accounted for by two blocks on materials, two on testing and research methods, one on language learning and teaching, one on methodology, and one on dissertation planning. The actual dissertations were expected to be done in the students' own time. The "student contribution" was to be accommodated by allocating half of every alternate period to assigned readings or discussion of directed questions.

For evaluation, four two-hour or three-hour examinations at mid-year and the end of the year would count for 900 marks. Another 900 marks would be allocated from a total of eleven "short assignments"—designing materials, presenting some aspect of methodology, and constructing a test—and a "dissertation." The short assignments were said to be "learning exercises" rather than opportunities to evaluate students, but the marks counted and there would be no marks for assignments submitted late. When joint authorship of an assignment was permitted, individual students were expected to indicate which parts they were responsible for so that tutors could allocate "fair credit" for individual work.

I listened to long discussions about the actual content to be included under the topic headings. Everyone wanted to put more into the course, but they could not agree on anything that might be given up. Some suggested, for example, that two blocks of phonology were excessive and that one would be adequate. They were told that the professor who regularly taught the two blocks would refuse to teach just one and that there was no one else to teach the topic.

SUCH A HEAVY REGIMEN of undiluted "transmission" teaching and passive learning seemed to me old-fashioned and inappropriate for any students, especially experienced graduates. I suggested that the students should not be treated simply as recipients of information. Weren't independent thought and initiative to be encouraged? I was told: "We know what is best for our students. There is no time to arrange anything different. There is no need to change."

My professional writings all argued against such a "top-down" approach to education. I did not believe mature graduate students had nothing to contribute from their own experiences. I expected my students to learn from each other as well as from me, and I would certainly learn from them, especially at the beginning, when it would be more important for me to listen than to lecture.

My colleagues were unable to contemplate this point of view. They saw it as disruptive and unproductive. We reached an impasse. I could see no reason why I should stay at the university. I did not see how I could teach in such a situation. I had nothing to contribute.

The discussion was emotional for us all. I had come to South Africa to be useful. I had not anticipated total frustration. The staff also felt they had a great investment in me. My appointment had been widely publicized, and it would not look good if the first head of the department decided that it was impossible to work with the rest of the staff. The funding for my position had been linked to me personally and would be lost. Everyone felt thwarted. In their shock and anger, my colleagues offered me the opportunity to demonstrate what I was arguing for: *"Show us what YOU would do!"*

I reiterated that I would build upon the expertise of the students.

How would I organize the course?

I could not say. I did not yet know the students. I did not know what would be useful to them. I did not know what they would contribute.

Then how would I proceed?

I would use the first quarter—the first seven weeks, just one eighth of the total course—so that instructors and students could plan the rest of the course together. I would leave the students to work out for themselves and recommend how they thought the course should be conducted—what would be most useful for them.

I would hand the course over to the students?

No. But I would give them an opportunity to express a point of view and to build on their own experience. I would give them seven weeks to come up with their own recommendations. I would empower them.

I felt that the students—whom I had not yet met, though I knew most of them would be experienced practising teachers in white schools and black schools—would not only benefit from the opportunity but that they would benefit us. Their conclusions would give us insights not only into the form and content of the Honours course in the future but into all the department's courses and into the proposed Centre for Applied English Language Studies as well. The students could help us discover what Applied English Language Studies should mean in a South African context.

The original decision to let things work for seven weeks as I suggested took courage on the part of my colleagues, who were not accustomed to relinquishing control. Or was it curiosity if not relief that reconciled them to taking a temporary spectator role? It was not until several weeks later that I learned the extent of the doubt, misgivings, and mistrust that some of them had.

At the time, I did not feel I was proposing anything particularly radical or out of line. I had been specifically invited to lead the department and to provide guidance, demonstrations, and the benefit of extensive overseas experience. My views of education, which urged respect for students at all levels, had been made public in more than a dozen books. I would not do anything that was not routinely done in graduate schools of education elsewhere in the world. I was confident.

WHEN I WENT OUTSIDE, waiting for the adrenalin rush to subside, I found the empty campus transformed. Registration had begun. A vibrant, colourful, smiling mass of polycultural, polyracial students was discovering itself.

Jostling groups were displaying what they had to share and exploring what others could share with them. There were stalls, posters, notices, demonstrations, entertainments, speeches, arguments, piquant food, enticing smells, and polyphonic music. The university was alive, renewed, and anticipatory. The atmosphere of promise had returned.

Chapter 2

Week Zero

It is perhaps fitting that the first Honours student I meet in the department comes to be tested. Although candidates with a relevant bachelor's degree and teaching experience are technically eligible for admission to the course, the Honours programme *begins* with a test of written English, which students can fail before they even start.

The rationale is that writing ability must be assessed because it will be essential to the conduct and outcome of the course—though it is not a course on writing and it is acknowledged that some of the students may never write again after they have completed the course. There is also an interview, which permits assessment of the quality of the candidates' spoken English. Part of the three-hour written test involves reading extracts from transformational grammar texts and doing "tree structure" analyses of simple sentences. Candidates are also asked to explain how they might use the rather outdated and esoteric art of constructing tree structures in their own teaching, a delicate question because the staff are divided on the utility of 1960s transformational grammar in contemporary English language pedagogy. In defence of tree structures, I am told that students have to be tested on something and that tree structures are ideal and impartial because black students like them and usually do well on them.

The first black student I meet is Albert—tall, tentative, and soft-spoken with fluent English. He is the head of the English department in a high school in Soweto, a tough job in a tough location. He tells me he was terrified of taking the test and trembled all the way through. I scoff, and he tells me that there is a great deal at stake for him and that black students expect to fail at tests. He says that a major reason for the huge drop-out rate among black high school students is the testing they are subjected to—not just the number of tests, but the high probability that the consequence will be another experience of failure. He tries to encourage students to stay in school, but testing drives them out. He hates tests.

It is a hot day, and Albert wears just a sweatshirt over a pair of green army slacks and sneakers. So also does Benjamin, who has had a long drive from Bophuthatswana, one of the fictitious "homelands" within South Africa that blacks have been actively encouraged to "return to" if they are not usefully employed in the mines or white metropolises. Benjamin is shorter and stockier than Albert, with a beaming round face, greying wavy hair, and spectacles. He is the acting principal of a high school and teaches English, Afrikaans, and Zulu. His drive to Wits from his home and school is over a hundred miles, and he asks if he might complete his part-time studies over a period of three years rather than two. He is turned down; it would be too much of a demand on the hard-worked staff, who cannot give individual students special treatment. There is also a suggestion that Benjamin would do better to give up immediately because his plan to commute is impractical. But he quietly, smilingly persists. He will manage. I realize what an enormous world-encompassing opportunity it must seem for black students to study at a white institution like Wits.

Albert and Benjamin are obviously experienced teachers with authority in their own domains and great motivation. But the group will also have its cadet members. I meet shy, diffident Faith, born in South Africa of Asian parents, who has just completed her undergraduate studies and has a temporary job in the university library. Faith's teaching experience is limited to informal English lessons to friends recently arrived from Asia, and she says her aim is to continue teaching in this way. Some of the staff are dubious. Is Faith merely looking for a course to take—to fill in time and pick up a qualification—before making a career decision? But her written and spoken English are impeccable, and she performs well on the test. She is admitted.

WE INTRODUCE OURSELVES, the Honours students and the staff, at an "orientation" session in the cluttered semibasement room in which the meetings of the course will be held. If we look up through the bars of the shallow windows at the back of the room, we can see the feet of hundreds of students moving in and out of an examination hall. The battered desk provided for the instructor in front of the chalkboard is covered by a white tablecloth set up by some of the instructors with earthenware goblets, wine, and wafers of cheese biscuits—rather like a sacramental altar—and also with some juice and sandwiches. It is friendly in a formal kind of way. People take their refreshments and sit at old steel and vinyl chairs behind steel and plywood tables around the perimeter of the room.

The instructors, who tend to cluster in a group, briefly state their names and teaching interests. According to my notes, I speak last and say something like this:

"My name is Frank, and I've come to Wits to help my colleagues here set up the new Department of Applied English Language Studies. But there's a problem. We're not really sure of everything that English language implies, the ways in which it is applied, and how it should be studied. We are expected to be useful in language education in the South Africa of today and tomorrow, and we certainly want to be useful or at least relevant. We're trying to find our way.

"One thing we are doing is setting up new courses in this mysterious area of Applied English Language Studies and reviewing courses that have been given for several years, like the present Honours course that you are now being welcomed to. This course has been given for many years and has continually been revised to better serve its purposes. When I arrived here a couple of months ago, the course was still under discussion even though we had a carefully worked-out teaching plan in front of us. On paper, it looked very neat, with squares for every teaching block, topic titles inside every square, and initials beside the titles to indicate who would teach the blocks. We were all ready to hand out copies to you.

"But we still had some questions. We weren't sure whether we needed to teach you everything on the teaching plan, and we weren't sure whether we hadn't left important matters off the plan. We weren't sure how much time we should spend teaching you the different topics, and we weren't sure how useful they would be to you. We weren't sure of the use *you* would make of the knowledge and skills we tried to give you.

"One thing we all believed was that our students should teach in a flexible manner. But our own teaching plan didn't seem very flexible. We all believed that *you* should make the needs and interests of your students the first teaching priority. We were not sure that we were making our own students' needs and interests the first priority. We didn't think we really knew what your needs and interests were. We believed that teaching should be research based. But we had no research behind our present teaching. We believed that teachers had to demonstrate the way they wanted their students to teach, but we weren't sure we would be setting a good example.

"We decided we didn't want to teach this course without involving you in the discussions and research necessary for coming to the best decisions. What we decided was to make the first seven weeks of this course an investigation into how the rest of it should be conducted. That was a decision we took without consulting you, but we were trapped by our own logic and time constraints. We decided—a second arbitrary decision—that we would make no more arbitrary decisions once the course had started.

"The next seven weeks, then, will be an exploration. We will as a group—staff and students, though we'll try to get rid of the distinction—try to decide what this Honours course should ideally be. We will—with your approval, I hope—examine the individual situations that each of you finds yourself in. We will talk about our own jobs, our own responsibilities, and our own pupils or students, as well as our own experience and motivations. Each of us in the group will know things the others don't know, and we will try to pool our knowledge about what the ideal balance of the course should be and how it should be taught. Of course, we won't know these answers immediately. We will all have to do research to find out. We will have to find evidence or at least good reasons for supporting the inclusion or exclusion of anything in the course.

"And we will have been through a useful exercise. We will, I hope, demonstrate a *professional,* collegial, collaborative approach to planning an educational venture based on reason, evidence, and sensitivity, not on whim or strength of conviction. We will, I hope, learn things useful not only to us but to others—not only to our students, but to our colleagues. We will, I hope, all be ready to think about disseminating—at some time, in some way—what we will learn during the coming seven weeks.

"The staff are not trying to abdicate any responsibilities here. We're not saying, 'Tell us what you want and we'll give it to you.' We are not asking you to negotiate a curriculum with us. We are not expecting you to learn by accident. We think we must keep the search going and give it direction when it falters. We are not asking you to learn by chance; our job is to help you learn. But we can do better if we can learn what you need to learn—if we all learn together.

"We recognize that we probably know more about some things than you do—that is part of our job. We all have our specialties. But you almost certainly know things that we don't know. And our job is to ensure that you teach us those things.

"Learning and teaching are a mutual enterprise, a search. Learning is not slabs of knowledge: It is the development of understanding. We want to demonstrate that to you and engage you in it."

THERE ARE SOME MOMENTS OF SILENCE. Then a student deferentially invites a visiting professor of linguistics to make the first response. "When do we applaud?" the professor asks ambiguously.

Guy, a slight, fair-haired, and pigtailed young man who is a part-time writer and artist and a part-time teacher of English and Afrikaans to older black students at home and in Soweto, declares: "This will be a *jol* (pronounced *jawl,* a ubiquitous South African term that means, at its most innocuous, party). It's so *lekker* (literally, delicious)."

Dark-haired Joanna, curled up raptly on her chair with a leg tucked beneath her, says to me: "Do you mean there won't be any handouts? What about reading lists?" Her dark eyes are intense and penetrating. A sometime colleague of Guy's, she teaches English part-time to black students in a white high school and also in the university. She is also a free-lance storyteller.

I say: "No handouts. No lists. I hope you'll all read. But you don't all have to read the same things." Joanna nods an encouraging acknowledgement, but her face is reserving judgment.

A student raises an important question: May she smoke? A staff member staidly responds that it is against university policy and that ambient smoke is detrimental to everyone's health.

Sitting together close to me are two impressive figures, majestically placid black matrons. I feel that if the course is to work, it has to have their approbation. One of them, Elizabeth, is a high school teacher in Soweto, like Albert. The other, Gertrude, has driven to the meeting over forty miles from a DET high school north of Pretoria. Gertrude says she is delighted that the class will not be "theory," like so many university courses. I warn her that the air will be thick with theories and that we will be breathing them all the time—until the university decides it is detrimental to everyone's health. I think she means she is delighted by the prospect of contributing to discussions, but I am mistaken. What Gertrude wants in place of "theory" is "practical" advice on how to teach English (which she has been teaching for years).

Joanna pointedly asks me what I expect to get out of the seven weeks.

I try to be candid: "A book. But you could get a book out of it too. I hope everyone will write at least one thing, individually or collaboratively, a book, an article for a popular or professional journal, a script . . . we should let other people know about this."

The students nod approval of this declaration, and no one objects, so I continue: "But I also want to get an interesting seven weeks out of it. I think I can spend a worthwhile couple of months with you all planning a worthwhile course, perhaps something that in the long run may help to change the way things are a little."

Brandon is small and slight—a silent-running dynamo. He teaches English in a "rural" DET secondary school, which means it is in one of the smaller black townships outside the cities. But he also teaches his own courses on language enrichment, societal values, and ideology to older students at a "pretechnical" institution. He dresses formally—jacket, white shirt, and tie, with heavy dark-rimmed spectacles under a furrowed ebony brow and carefully parted hair—but a frequent, almost mischievous smile lights his face when he talks. He is another soft speaker, so you have to concentrate to hear him. His first comment is typical: "Don't the group think they might find it difficult having to go back to the 'old style' of classes after seven weeks?" I say that perhaps they will decide not to go back to the old style.

Brandon is also concerned about my credentials: "Tell us how you got here." He accepts a brief autobiography.

I am concerned about Elizabeth, sitting so silently and monumentally beside me, and ask what she thinks about it all.

Elizabeth thinks, while I wait for a conventional response or even no response. Then suddenly, firmly, she says: "I wish there'd been something like this when I started teaching eighteen years ago." Gertrude nods equally firmly, and my afternoon is made.

Naturally, the "evaluation" question comes up. Several students want to know how they will be marked. I say they can discuss that during the seven weeks, but I have no plans to evaluate them at all.

My colleagues, the instructors, watch and say nothing.

A FEW DAYS LATER, I have a corridor encounter with a colleague who has participated in a conference workshop where the question of "students negotiating their own learning" was discussed and it was concluded that, in general, it did not make very much difference. I say that students in the Honours course are not negotiating anything—an activity I see as slipping a bit of additional responsibility onto students without giving them any corresponding authority or influence. But my colleague insists that although "negotiating the curriculum" might not be the best term—a matter discussed at the conference—it is as good as any other. It's the same idea, isn't it? The colleague asks where it would be possible to read more about what I am doing with the group. I say that what is taking place will be unique to this particular group. There are no general rules as far as I know.

"So where can I read about it?" my colleague persists. "It must be written up somewhere."

Chapter 3

Shadows

South Africa is a nation that has never been whole, dogged by a history of repression and coercion that seems to have entered people's bones. It is like a lake poisoned by countless sources of pollution.

Blacks live with an inescapable legacy of white exploitation of their labour, with hated passes that symbolised their subjugation, "influx laws" that limited where they could live and travel, the enforced breakup of families, low wages, abysmal living conditions, a brutal reaction to any protest, constant public and private humiliation, detention without reason or recourse, imprisonment, torture, banishment, death, and bloody intergroup rivalries leaving a trail of misery that persists today in the highest murder rate in the world.

Afrikaners, descendants of the original Dutch and Huguenot settlers, have their own history as subjects of violence—at the hands of black warriors who bloodily disputed control of territory with them and of the British who wanted to colonize the entire country themselves. The Afrikaners made their epic and bloody *voortreks* a century and a half ago to preserve their own independent way of life, their culture, and their language. They fought two bitter "wars of independence" against the British at the turn of the present century, with guerilla resistance that brought savage "scorched earth" reprisals and the world's first concentration camps upon them and their families. They believed they had biblical warrant for what they saw as their rights and duties in South Africa: to live in a state of "apartness" (apartheid) from everyone else. Today, Afrikaners are the largest group of voters in the country, with total control of the government—until blacks are enfranchised.

The British have lost the political power they once had—as they lost South Africa from their Commonwealth in 1961—but they still have overriding economic power in the country, strengthened by sentiments of superiority that come with an imperial heritage and a language of international standing. Like the Afrikaners, South Africans of British origin see themselves with merited authority and deeply established roots in the country—and with a dark and doubtful future.

And beyond the scars of conflict, there is in all South Africans a great pride and feeling for the rich and scenic country itself, which drives each group to strive to own and mold the land as they see best.

There are about 10 million whites in the country, speaking mainly Afrikaans (6.2 million) and English (3.4 million), plus a smattering of other European languages and virtually no African languages. There are about 30 million blacks speaking varieties of ten African languages, mainly Zulu (8.5 million) and Xhosa (nearly 7 million). Almost a quarter of the black population—about 7 million people—live in squatters camps. Most of the about 3 million coloureds speak Afrikaans, and something under 1 million Indians speak mainly English. No black African language reaches across the entire nation, and Afrikaans has great national but limited international influence.

In 1910, English and Dutch (later Afrikaans) became the two "official" languages of the country. Afrikaans, which derives from the language of original Dutch settlers (and which Afrikaners now regard as an indigenous "African language" representing the identity of the nation), is the major language of government, equal to if not dominant over English in education, broadcasting, and other national arenas. Afrikaans is highly unpopular with almost everyone who is not Afrikaner because of its association with apartheid. Both Afrikaans and English (and a choice of vernacular African language) must be taught in all schools and are part of all matriculation examinations.

Languages are continually changing, rising and falling, in South Africa as everywhere else in the world. A language known as *Fanakalo* developed in mining areas and is a corrupt and diminished form of vernacular languages consisting primarily of commands and instructions. Mining companies have formally abolished its use, but the companies still decide which languages should be used in work situations. In black township areas, people from different linguistic backgrounds have developed their own languages in order to communicate. They are extremely multilingual, and there is much "code switching" between different languages and dialects. There is a language of the teenage township gangs, called (in a blend of Zulu and Afrikaans) *tsotsi-taal*.

By the year 2000, fewer than 4 per cent of the South African population will be native speakers of English. Estimates put illiteracy among blacks in South Africa today at around 50 per cent—about the same as their estimated level of unemployment. But language, educational, and social research have long been limited in South Africa because of international academic protests

against apartheid (Young, 1987). South African educators often do not realize that many teachers in Britain, North America, and elsewhere have had
long experience at working in multiracial and multilingual classrooms with all
kinds of social and even violent problems. And after years of international
opprobrium, it is difficult for South African educators to respond to outside
help, advice, and even inquiry without resentment and suspicion.

THE DISCRIMINATORY CATEGORIES are bureaucratic inventions. *Blacks* is a
general term that embraces a variety of African ethnic groupings or their
relics. *Indians* refers to Malays and other Asians often originally brought into
the country as slaves. *Coloureds* are the descendants of a variety of racial
mixes. Unlike the unenfranchised majority blacks, those in Indian and
coloured categories have been given a vote and limited political representa-
tion. But to attempt to determine the real "racial origin" of any individual
whose family tree goes back more than a few generations in South Africa
would be a pointless exercise, though it occupied a mad bureaucracy for years
and still survives on many official forms. One student told me her three children had been registered as having different ethnic origins from each other.

Many official and departmental documents at the University of the Witwatersrand required students to state their mother tongue, which was an
oblique way of determining racial classification.

Until recent years, the word *bantu* (people) was extensively and erro-
neously used by whites to refer to black Africans. *Bantustans* were areas of the
country declared to be "tribal homelands" of blacks, to which entire popula-
tions were moved. The homelands and the concept behind them remain, but
the word bantu has gone out of favour.

The Bantu Education Act of April 1955 passed control of black education
from provinces (and missions) to the Department of Bantu Education (later,
the DET), with total control of teachers, pupils, and syllabuses. It became a
criminal offence to run a school that had not been recognized by the department, and children who did not report to the department's schools would be
banned from further schooling for life.

A minister of native affairs and later prime minister, Hendrik Verwoerd,
spelt out the underlying philosophy in a notorious speech in the South
African Senate on 7 June 1954, a paradigmatic example of the apartheid
mind:

> There is no place for the Bantu in the European community above the level
> of certain forms of labour. . . . It is of no avail for him to receive a train-
> ing which draws him away from his own community and misleads him by
> showing him the green pastures of the Europeans but still does not allow
> him to graze there. . . . This leads to the much-discussed frustration of

educated natives who can find no employment which is acceptable to them
. . . it must be replaced by planned Bantu education . . . with its roots
entirely in native areas and in the native environment and community.

In 1961, violence was met by violence with the formation of umKhonto
we Sizwe (abbreviated as MK and meaning spear of the nation), the armed
wing of the ANC. In 1963, almost the entire ANC leadership, including Nelson Mandela, was arrested on charges of sabotage and sentenced to life
imprisonment, served mostly on Robben Island in the Atlantic Ocean off
Cape Town. The island became known as ANC college because of the number of educated blacks segregated there and the "each one teach one" philosophy they developed.

On 16 June 1976, 20,000 schoolchildren marched in Soweto to demonstrate against a decree by the Department of Bantu Education that Afrikaans
should be used as a medium of instruction in secondary schools equally with
English, even though many teachers could not function in Afrikaans. To
learn mathematics, black students had to learn Afrikaans as well as English.
The student protest met a violent response, and in just over a week 176 people were killed. The first to die was a thirteen-year-old schoolboy, shot from
behind. Other children even younger were killed. Work boycotts, school
boycotts, school burnings, reprisals, and further killings followed and spread
nationwide, accompanied by unlimited police powers of entry and detention, torture, political jailings, deportations, and the smashing of families
and communities. The students won a pyrrhic victory, and Afrikaans was
withdrawn from the curriculum. But black education was in a shambles from
which it has scarcely begun to recover, especially as township violence and
the gross inequities (or absence) of all social services for blacks have continued. The widespread breakdown and the historic disparities have left students at all levels with a disturbed and impoverished educational background and with a substantial lack of training and professionalism among
black teachers.

It was estimated that over a million black children had received no education at all. Many others had been to school for short periods only. Fewer
than 10 per cent of school dropouts got work. There were many violent
teenage gangs preying more on blacks in townships than on whites. There
was an enormous absence of literacy among blacks. Whites explained: "They
don't come from a culture of literacy."

DESPITE THE SHOW OF HARMONY between de Klerk and Mandela at the
Codesa talks, including some carefully orchestrated public skirmishes to
demonstrate their independence, it was clear that each walked a fine political

line. One was concerned with the most he would be allowed to concede at the talks, and the other with the least he would be allowed to accept. Each trailed an ominous shadow.

The shadow behind Mandela was his strongest black political opponent, Zulu Chief Mangosuthu Buthelezi, whose Inkatha Freedom Party was boycotting the talks and continuing to be involved in frequent bloody incidents with ANC supporters, who were mainly of Xhosa origin. Buthelezi claimed that the ANC was ingratiating itself too much with the white government and was selling out blacks. But the Inkatha Party was in disrepute because of evidence that it had received substantial support to foment discord among blacks from the white-controlled South African Defence Force. The state president had been aware of this, but no one knew in how much detail. He had given assurances that there would be no more dirty tricks, but these were only words.

The shadow behind de Klerk was the white right-wing Conservative Party, which had become the country's official opposition as the National Party moved to the centre in its efforts to reach an accommodation with the ANC. The National Party had absorbed so many liberals that the weakened left-wing Democratic Party lost its role as official opposition, making the Conservative Party not only politically stronger but more conspicuous and more threatening. The Conservatives were boycotting Codesa and were developing ties with even more extreme white ideological groups.

The violence of blacks against blacks was growing, especially in the crowded townships north and south of Johannesburg. Interracial violence was still rare, except for some gruesome and highly publicized black attacks on white teachers in rural areas, which reflected perhaps frustration with abysmal educational conditions, and the murders of whites on remote farms by groups of blacks, which were isolated tragedies without apparent political implications. But there was a looming threat of violence from the extreme white right: Afrikaners with a bitter history of struggle for total control of part of South Africa if not of the entire country and for the apartheid that went with this control.

There was atavistic talk of a need for a "white homeland" where Afrikaners could freely exercise their right to live apart from all other groups except under their own terms. Their authority could be found in writing, in the Bible. Nightly television broadcasts showed an army of men and women in uniforms and insignia redolent of Nazi Germany, openly drilling for the bloodbath and civil war that they said would surely arrive the day South Africa was handed over to blacks. Seeds of anger and resentment sown in the past might sprout and flourish anywhere at any time.

Against this background of political and social uncertainty, Codesa moved into closed commission sessions where constitutional planning was to take place. For many of those shut outside, not knowing what was going on was a loss of control worse than any clear outcome might be.

UNEXPECTEDLY, THE GOVERNMENT SUMMARILY ANNOUNCED a dramatic restructuring of the white educational system, widely interpreted as preempting any possibility that a Codesa agreement could open white schools unrestrictedly to blacks.

The existing system, a masterpiece of bureaucratic ingenuity, classified white schools into four "models." Model A schools were completely private and could essentially make up their own rules and regulations. Model B schools were state operated, with management committees that had some control over admissions, provided they did not exclude any white student living in the area of the school and kept the student body at least 51 per cent white. In Model C schools, management committees of local parents had responsibility for everything except teachers' salaries, paid by the government. The small number of Model D schools were new with no fixed black: white ratio, and became almost entirely black.

The new decision was that henceforth all state schools would be designated Model C, in effect privatizing education. All school buildings, formerly public property, would be handed over to local management groups. The government would pay teachers' salaries to a limited extent—although 4,000 teachers could lose their jobs as an immediate consequence. Funds for everything else, including additional teachers, would have to be found by the parents. The decision obviously favoured rich districts over poor districts. The decision also consolidated apartheid in schools, as local management groups would determine admissions. "White schools" could become whiter; "black schools" would remain unrelievedly black. Several students in the Honours group in the Department of Applied English Language Studies might be personally affected, and the entire group was disturbed.

AN ORIENTATION SESSION WAS HELD at the university for new staff. Thirty men and women from many parts of the world—but no black South Africans— were apprised of the university's continuing dedication to cutbacks, constraint, cost-effectiveness, excellence, and the preservation of standards. All this would be achieved by the streamlining of operations, rigorous bookkeeping, and the maintenance of high pass marks in examinations. Senior university administrators acknowledged a responsibility to train the future leaders of South Africa, but those future leaders would have to meet the academic standards of Wits if they wanted to have the experience of Wits. Everything academically would be done to help them, but the demonstration of leadership qualities could not in itself be regarded as an adequate student contribution. Degrees so arduously earned by white students could not be devalued by alternative criteria that increased the probability that blacks might get them. It was suggested that the quality of the total experience that the university could offer all its students might be considered as important as the specific academic competencies that students were expected to demonstrate. The responses were immediate: We can't give degrees for nothing, we refuse to dilute the quality of our degrees, we reject the philosophy of "pass one, pass all."

The first-year failure rate among black students at Wits was 23 per cent. A young black woman told me: "In my community, I'm a leader. At Wits, I'm a failure."

At a meeting of the university senate the following day, there was discussion of a controversial new high school curriculum plan produced by a government commission. A mathematics professor thought there was too much emphasis on language in the plan at the expense of mathematics and science (fewer than 1,000 black students a year were matriculating in mathematics in the entire country). Another professor was concerned about a bias toward vocational education at the expense of more academic kinds of learning. It was noted that the plan did not take into account differences in the circumstances under which people came into education. But most of the discussion was abstract, as if the problem was academic and not social and political.

I GAVE MY FIRST CLASS in the new second-year course. In addition to about eighty undergraduate students, rather more black than white, there were academic staff from my own and other departments. The general topic was language and education, and my particular focus was on thinking and learning. The point I wanted to make was that learning without thinking was senseless if not impossible but that thinking always resulted in learning. I discussed a variety of theoretical positions relevant to this issue. I asserted that students should come to university for the opportunity to think—not to be told what they should learn or blindly memorize. They should accept the responsibility of deciding for themselves between the positions of different "experts," evaluating for themselves what instructors or the authors of books told them, and pursuing their own lines of thought. I said that independent inquiry was more important than reading lists. I also said there were professors who believed that "some students" could not think or that it was wrong to "confuse students" by telling them there might be conflicting points of view. The lecture seemed well received by some students and by some staff. Others, of course, did not comment.

In the smaller tutorial group immediately afterwards, I was more explicit. I said that it was black students who were thought incompetent, sometimes even by black professors. A black student very quietly but very pointedly asked me: "Don't you think then that black students have the right to protest?" I fudged, sensing that there might be more to the question than I understood. I said that everyone should oppose stereotyping in any form. But the student was clearly disappointed with my response and stayed silent for the rest of the session.

Afterwards, a young white student told me helpfully that I should watch my tongue. A colleague had already indicated this. But how can one talk if one must watch one's tongue? It would take me years to even begin to understand the intricacies of politically correct talk in South Africa. Was this a place where there was apartheid in opening your mouth—where words must be separated from thoughts?

THERE WAS A BY-ELECTION at the rural centre of Potchefstroom. It was anticipated that de Klerk's National Party candidate would be defeated by the Conservatives, but not by the 8,000 votes that made the eventual difference. White paranoia and racial passions seemed to have determined the outcome. The country was told that the rest of the world thought the new South Africa would be a land of violence, not of harmony.

A day later, de Klerk announced that he would hold an all-white referendum. Whites would decide by ballot who would represent them at the Codesa talks. In principle, the question would be who would lead South Africa through the coming changes: the "moderate and conciliatory" National Party or the intransigent and belligerent Conservatives? If de Klerk lost, he and his government would resign. The poll was regarded as a gamble that de Klerk had to take if he was to retain authority. But the stakes were high for the country as well as for himself. If he won, he could consolidate his position in the public's eyes at least (including, of course, all the onlooking but still unenfranchised blacks). But if he lost, white extremists could become the next government, Codesa would certainly collapse, and South Africa would be back in the throes of overt interracial conflict.

Departmental Dialogues

Have you considered doing this?
> It wouldn't work here.

It works everywhere else.
> But this is South Africa.

You want students to learn to think, don't you?
> Of course. But you can't put doubts into their minds. They can't handle it. So you have to tell them what's best.

May I tell you how an outsider sees the situation?

Why not wait until you've been here six months?

In six months, I'll be thinking like a South African.

Exactly.

Couldn't there be more contact between the department and teachers in the field?

The university is very dubious about diploma programmes.

Don't give diplomas.

Then black teachers wouldn't come.

Go to them.

They don't want people dropping in to tell them what they're doing wrong.

Let's do some research. Give half the students the usual component of grammar and phonology, but let the rest do a lot of independent reading and writing instead. That way, we can find out if the grammar and phonology really make a difference.

The students wouldn't stand for it. It wouldn't be fair to those deprived of the grammar and phonology.

But we don't know that the deprivation will be harmful to them
There's no evidence it does them any good. This way, we'd find out.

We don't need to find out. This is the way we've always done it.

Are all these photocopied handouts necessary?

Students must all have a chance to learn.

Must they all learn the same things?

How could we mark them if they didn't?

Couldn't students do more free reading?

Not if it interferes with their course work.

What if we encourage them to read in their own time?

They would spend less time on their assignments.

But how will students ever come to read independently?

They won't. They don't come from a culture of literacy.

Couldn't students be allowed more initiative?

    Black students expect to be told what to do.

Why do they expect that?

    They've always been told what to do.

Suppose we refuse to tell them?

    We have to respect their traditions.

The Honours Students

DET Teachers

Albert	Department head, secondary school, Soweto
Benjamin	Acting principal, secondary school, Bophuthatswana
Bonnie	Primary school teacher, Soweto
Brandon	Rural secondary school teacher
Elizabeth	Secondary school teacher, Soweto
Gertrude	Rural school teacher

Others

Alice	University lecturer
Charles	Secondary school lecturer, Johannesburg
Deirdre	Department head, alternative school, Johannesburg
Eleanor	Department head, intermediate school, Johannesburg
Faith	Chinese South African, part-time teacher
Guy	Writer, artist, part-time teacher
Joanna	Storyteller, part-time teacher
Laura	Project head, upgrade school for Alexandra students
Marina	University lecturer
Mavis	College of education lecturer
Thomas	College of education lecturer

Chapter 4

Week One

MONDAY

This is the first day of seven weeks of a totally new experience for students in the Honours programme of the Department of Applied English Language Studies. They will, I hope, review their own and South Africa's educational concerns and experiences, decide what would be the most relevant kind of course for them to participate in, share their insights and decisions with the staff—and the world will change. If it doesn't, mud will be on my face and an opportunity will be lost for something worthwhile and different to be demonstrated. For the next seven weeks, all course decisions will be made by the students. This will be more than an academic exercise; they will have power. There is not even a plan for the first day.

But the week has to get started. Expectations may be different, but we begin in the customary fashion. We begin by sitting and looking at each other.

I have ignored the unoccupied instructor's table and sit among a cluster of students at one side of the room, waiting for something to happen. But the students wait for me or for one of the other four staff members in the room to start talking. It is a question of who can tolerate the silence least. With everyone looking to me, I capitulate. I say there are organizational matters to be discussed. The students attend deferentially.

I have brought a plan—just in case. There are supposed to be afternoon classes, every day from Monday to Thursday. Nothing on Friday afternoons. I propose hours of 4:00 P.M. to 5:30 P.M., with a prompt start (to encourage people to arrive on time), a flexible finish (to encourage people to stay), and no formal break. There are immediately scheduling problems. Marina and Alice can't come on Monday afternoons because they have university teaching commitments of their own at that time.

They are also already aggrieved over another matter. Other students think it will be difficult to come in on Wednesdays for departmental seminars on language and learning that the staff think students should attend. We do the best we can. Students agree to my suggestion that Monday should be a "free day," when those who can might come to work in groups or to do "research" in the library or elsewhere. Wednesday will be a seminar day for those who can make it, and Tuesday and Thursday will be formal meeting days when everyone should be present though they may decide to meet in small groups. I object on principle to having an attendance register, though most of the students expect it and some think it desirable.

Students exchange names, interests, information about where they teach, and if their schools would be open for visits from the rest of us— my suggestion again. Most of the students would like to make visits and to receive them; it is a novel idea for them. The black students would particularly like white teachers to visit their schools, but not at the moment. There is too much bloodshed around the townships. Laura offers to coordinate the visits, with help from a couple of others. A slight, decisive woman, Laura gave up a senior position in a white school a couple of years ago to open a part-time "educational upgrade" school where bright township children are helped to adapt to the ways of the white schools they might get opportunities to go to. This is quite unusual. The Honours students are clearly a special company.

I suggest they form "committees" to collect documentation, to keep track of things to be done, and to invite staff and outside visitors to "present evidence" if required. Pairs of students eventually volunteer to look after these committee assignments, but nothing comes of them. This is not what they are waiting for. The students write their names, schools, and telephone numbers for me to circulate. Charles, a businesslike English teacher in a white high school, comments on his slip that he "hates committees."

One person does show initiative. Brandon says they will need coffee and tea, and he will take care of the arrangements. He makes the offer without sounding subservient. We are relaxed and comfortable with one another.

A dean who has expressed some interest—or concern?—about what we are doing pays a call. I invite the students to explain what is going on. A few respond hesitantly, but I think they make a good job of it. The dean claims to have done a similar thing some years ago in an undergraduate class, where students were allowed to select any topic they wanted for a term paper. There was a surprisingly good selection of topics and quality of papers, the dean says. I do not see our seven-week course-planning enterprise as anything like students choosing their own topic for a paper. But the dean is satisfied to have found a cognitive peg—a convenient classification—for our enterprise.

We run into more organisational problems. Six members of the class—Faith, Guy, Joanna, and Charles, together with Deirdre and Eleanor whom I haven't yet heard speak—are full-time students. They are supposed to have meetings in the mornings as well as in the afternoons. The question is what they can do in the mornings that will be relevant to what they are doing in the afternoons with the part-time students. Moreover, eight part-time students will be deciding what the second year of their programme ought to be, but for the full-time students there will be no second year.

The provisional solution is that another staff member will conduct a morning language–learning and language–teaching seminar for the full-time students, who will examine under more organized conditions teaching experiences of their own that have been particularly helpful or particularly unhelpful. Their conclusions might be fed into the afternoon session, which will in any case probably consider similar matters. The problem is that the full-time students feel they should have some *particular* kind of additional experience—some "course content"—and that they will be missing important things if nothing specific is arranged for them. But they have a point. In particular, something must be done to prepare them for doing a dissertation, which the part-timers won't have to worry about until next year. Of course, the full-time students will still have the other three quarters of the present year to do something different, if they can overcome the feeling that they are just "marking time" for the first quarter.

The problem is even more acute with three students who began part-time studies last year—Marina and Alice, the young students who are already university instructors, and Thomas, who teaches at a college of education. They complain that they are forgotten people, and they are right. They were overlooked when the decision was made to allow the new intake of students to plan their own course. These students are not too happy with the programme they had last year, and they are jealous of what they view as special treatment for this year's students. They were also expecting to do some specific course work related primarily to the methodology of producing dissertations. This is an important matter, and something practical must be done for them immediately, both to reduce their anxieties and to make up for their feelings of neglect.

I would be happy if the afternoon sessions became so research oriented that they would cover much of the dissertation issue, although the students would still need specific guidance from faculty advisers. I receive reluctant, dubious agreement to postpone firm decisions for a while; these are clearly central considerations for the students.

In general conversation, the students begin to disclose a few of their particular interests and concerns. Brandon drops a small bombshell by

saying he would like to learn about high school students who are not
very intelligent—who are not smart enough to learn what they are taught
at school and are "destined to fail."

The remark draws a predictable reaction about the labelling of students with difficulties. Albert, the test hater, says the damage inflicted on
students is cumulative. Students who fail one year will almost certainly
fail the next, and inadequately educated students become inadequate
teachers. Teachers at all levels of education teach in the way they were
taught, he says.

There is discussion about the difficulty of changing teachers' attitudes
and teaching habits. Several people have commented on the "constraints"
on teachers. Deirdre is head of the ESL department of an "alternative"
school in a white Johannesburg suburb for students from Soweto. She
likes people to define their terms and wants to know what exactly these
constraints are. She teaches in exactly the way she wants to teach, she
says. She doesn't feel constrained in any way. She is given a catalogue of
constraints: the matric exams that all students must take, mandated syllabuses, other teachers, parents, and everything being driven by tests.

The relation of examinations to culture and society comes up. Brandon, whose particular concern is the self-perceptions of black students,
refers to specific constraints set by the DET, which prescribes texts and
even poems. The texts teach that blacks are employees and whites are
employers, says Brandon.

The class breaks up early—there is no further business to transact—but
no one is in a hurry to leave. There are still some students who have yet to
speak, whom I have not really met—like Mavis, Eleanor, and Bonnie.

TUESDAY

I am delayed on departmental business and arrive two minutes late to
find that everyone else has taken to heart my adjuration that we should
start promptly. The students and some visiting staff have taken every seat
in the room around the horseshoe arrangement of tables, leaving me only
one very conspicuous place at the isolated table at the head of the room.
The *teacher's* place. Was this an accident, a misplaced courtesy, or a
symbolic gesture? Is this how they see me despite my attempts—my
pleas—for a democratic approach?

People are chatting animatedly with each other when I come in,
which is good. They don't stop chatting when I take my place—also
good. At least they do not think that the arrival of the "teacher" demands
silence. In fact, they ignore me, and I clumsily interrupt them and in
effect demand silence (something I will not do again, but I am learning

my way as well), followed by a useless apology and unnecessary explanation for my lateness (which they don't care about). I don't think I can
launch immediately into some remarks that I have prepared, so I ask if
anyone has any comments "before we begin."

Joanna is again ready for me, tense and astute. She says there is concern
and uncertainty about where the class is going. She doesn't think it a good
idea that we just visit schools and share "experiences." The class is too big,
and one or two people will dominate it—are already dominating it. And of
course, she is right. She wants to know what my "agenda" is, which gives
me an opportunity to say what I intended to say in the first place.

I say that I have no agenda beyond what I had first outlined to them:
that the students should design what they thought would be the most
appropriate course. In the process, of course, I expected that they would
learn a great deal about their own schools, about educational needs in
South Africa, and about thinking through problems for themselves. Joanna
just looks at me; she obviously feels there is more but cannot say what it is
any more than I can divine what her concern might be. Silence follows,
with students waiting for me to talk next.

I elaborate on my "free Mondays" plan. I shall be there to talk with anyone who wants to talk to me, but I'll take a book in case no one comes. The
students can use the time in any way they want; I trust them. These organizational matters are really things the students should decide. I don't even
want to put ideas into their heads. I am a learner in South Africa as much as
they are. I will attend the meetings to learn, not to teach. This statement
seems to be well received, but it doesn't move the discussion along.

I have prepared for my own purposes some ideas on "resources" that
are available to the students and on questions they might address themselves to. I thought these ideas might be useful in the discussion at some
point. To break the silence again, I put two lists on the board. Under the
heading "Resources," I write:

1. Students' own experience
2. Observations of their own and other classrooms
3. The library
4. Staff.

Under the heading "Things to look for," I list (as examples):

How teachers talk to students, and students to each other
The kind of instruction and evaluation taking place
The formality of classes and schools
How bright the students are [picking up Brandon's inquiry]
Constraints on teachers [picking up Deirdre's inquiry].

In my organizational way, I suggest the students might consider allocating at least two people to monitor matters such as these, trying to
uncover implicit theories of language and learning that underlie all
teaching situations, the interpersonal relationships among teachers and
students, and the consequences for learning and thinking.

It all falls with a dull thud. There is no comment. Everyone still seems
to be waiting for something more definite to happen.

I don't want to make the next move, or to suggest it, or even to tell the
students once more that they must make the next move. There is a wall of
silence between us. I tell the students I am going for a coffee and walk out
of the room.

I am told later that the students were shocked and "galvanized into
action" by my abrupt departure. They had never before been left to their
own devices by an instructor. There was some recognition of my
dilemma—my need to get action started without initiating it—and even a
suggestion that it took some courage to leave the class as I did. I think it
was a desperate and lucky hunch.

Two of my colleagues are with the students at the time of my with-
drawal, and it leaves them in an invidious situation. Although there are
supposed to be no student-staff distinctions, they know that if they participate in the student discussions they will finish up dominating them. But
eventually they do participate—they participate and they dominate. The
staff always do. That will be a problem: The staff and students revert to
their traditional roles when they are together, the students looking for
guidance and evaluation and the staff providing it.

Brandon again demonstrates initiative. Shortly after I leave the room,
he takes the opportunity to collect the tea and coffee money.

I RETURN TWENTY MINUTES LATER to find the students organized into smaller
groups, all busily doing something. No one volunteers to explain anything
to me or even pays any particular attention to me. I read a book, learning
not to interrupt. Eventually, Laura invites me to join her group. They are
writing individual "questions" on slips of paper, which they then discuss—
a busywork activity, I uncharitably think, especially as the questions seem
to me far too broad and unfocused, like "How do we teach ESL?" or "How
can we improve grammar?" If the other groups are doing the same kind of
thing, we are just losing a day.

But at least people are talking to one another, and perhaps more is
happening than is apparent to me.

I learn later that the smaller groups have roughly sorted themselves
into four broad thematic areas:

Language and power—Joanna and Guy

Language and thought (the cognition group)—Marina, Alice, and
Thomas

Skills (reading, writing, speaking, and listening)—Albert, Benjamin,
Brandon, Elizabeth, Gertrude, and Mavis (a quietly persistent
teacher of English at a white college of education, whose constant
concern will be the "classroom mechanics" of language)

Language acquisition (first- and second-language learning)—Charles,
Laura, Deirdre, Faith, Eleanor (who I have learned teaches English
and Bible education in a white inner-city high school), and Bonnie
(who teaches English and science in a black school adjacent to
Soweto).

The groups are not fixed in composition or content, and there will be
movement between the two larger clusters especially, but in general they
will coalesce for the remaining weeks. The areas the groups have gone
into represent primary interests of the entire class rather than particular
interests of individuals, except perhaps for Joanna and Guy. Last year's
students—Marina, Alice, and Thomas—clearly prefer to stay together,
but otherwise there are no evident cliques.

I TALK WITH TWO OF MY COLLEAGUES about patching together a timetable so
that last year's students will not feel neglected. They will have the formal
classes on methodology and testing and on language learning and language teaching that they feel they must have—since they were on last
year's syllabus—but only in the second and third quarters of the year.
They will still be able to attend the afternoon sessions. We explain what
we propose, and to my relief the students are satisfied—once we block in
some labels on a timetable. There is one offer they do not accept. I propose including a session for them on language policy and language planning, perhaps the most burning issue in South African education today.
But they say they did that last year.

THURSDAY

Everyone is sitting around the horseshoe once again, waiting for the
large-group proceedings to begin. I manage to sit at the side this time and
do not say anything. There is a long silence.

   I don't know what anyone is thinking in the class (as I shall call the
large group). This is a problem for me. I still don't know if they will

move—if they can move—towards the construction of a useful, reasoned course proposal. A lot is at stake. I don't know why I don't completely trust seventeen bright and experienced people to do such a thing. I suppose it is the fear that everything will get out of control unless I control it myself—that the others will let me down. This is the fear that I feel infects all my colleagues in the department.

I am suspicious of my colleagues, as I know they are of me. They are coming to many of the sessions individually to huddle with groups of students who listen to them respectfully. I suspect the staff are already urging the students to include certain topics in their recommendations for the course, telling them that certain areas ought to be "covered." I am already concerned that the students in the groups they have formed are focusing less on their own experiences and interests than on what they have learned university courses look like. Already there have been requests for detailed information about last year's programme and about what the staff had planned for this year.

The first exchanges don't make me feel any better. Alice, one of the two young university instructors, suddenly tells the group she feels cynical about the visits to schools. Do they have any purpose beyond the appearance of things? She ticks off her objections. Do we know what we want to find out? Will we discover anything without several weeks of continuous observation? Don't teachers behave differently when observers are in the classroom? Is this anything more than a gesture?

Others suggest putting video cameras into classrooms or interviewing teachers, pupils, or parents. Deirdre produces a long journal article that details how difficult and unreliable classroom observation is. Elizabeth says there is a continuing problem with violence in her school.

But others counter the objections. Observation need not disrupt the classroom. Visitors—not more than one to a class—can come in, be quietly introduced, and sit unobtrusively among the students. Several of us have done exactly that in many different schools. It does not seem to be a great distraction. Most teachers are proud of the way they teach and blithely carry on the way they usually do, no matter what the observer might be thinking (provided the observer is not an evaluator). And information would be lost if we did not personally go into classrooms ourselves.

Perhaps the observers could also be observed, someone suggests, to discover whether they do indeed change the usual classroom procedures. Perhaps the observer of the observer, someone else suggests, could be a pupil who was one of the observed.

THE FOUR GROUPS BEGIN to make initial reports to one another about the kinds of questions they think the Honours course in future might usefully consider. Hesitantly, Mavis begins. (What is she so nervous about? She is an experienced teacher of adults and a mature and outgoing person, yet she is reluctant to put her own educational views forward before a staff member, although she is not slow to ask questions. Who taught her that her main role is to *listen?*) Mavis's group, which selected skills for its focus, seems primarily concerned with what teachers should do in classrooms. But they suggest using the questions that are being raised for self-reflection and for examination of "specifically South African issues" such as multicultural classrooms and the political basis of evaluation. (I later point out that such issues are hardly unique to South Africa. In Toronto and Vancouver, it is not unusual to find English spoken by fewer than 50 per cent of the children who arrive in school each year, with up to a hundred other languages being spoken in the same school. This comes as a surprise.)

Mavis's group suggests making all the different aspects of the investigation into small research projects, which might be put together into a kind of booklet. The group has a very practical orientation and would like to see the results in writing. The group also suggests bringing people in to discuss the topic of evaluation, such as matriculation examiners. They see a clash between teachers and "the system."

They want to know what the essential grammar and phonology knowledge is for teaching and learning English, as if a simple answer exists that could be made available to them. They are also interested in "the relationship between reading, writing, speaking, and listening in first and second language." There are many important issues here, but the group talks as if this is all "information" that exists somewhere, rather than constantly shifting aspects of situations in which they always have to work.

They also want to study South Africa's language policy. Someone suggests the desperate alternative of Esperanto as a language that everyone would have to learn from scratch. Class, dialect, and access to power are other topics that the group thinks are important.

Joanna and Guy have different approaches to second-language teaching, grammar, and first-language learning, which reflect their more recent experiences as students in formal course work at the university. They want to look at how first-language knowledge might interfere with the learning of subsequent languages and at "interlanguage," which some theorists have proposed as an intermediate stage between one language and another. They are concerned about the nature of error and of teachers' responses to it. They also want to know whether there are different "cognitive scaffolds" for different languages and whether different languages drive thought in different ways.

They want to examine assumptions about language and teaching and about respect for language in classrooms, and they are concerned with

how good the cross-section of schools is that they might visit. Laura
assures them: "Quite good."

Joanna says that she and Guy also want to examine historical and
political aspects of different streams of linguistic thought and the difference between semiotic and acquisition approaches to language learning.
How should the students position themselves pedagogically? Are they
doing what they want to be doing?

Deirdre anxiously intervenes to complain that jargon words are being
used, like *cognition, scaffolding,* and *acquisition.* What does *semiotics*
mean? There is a lot of discussion about this. Class members who have
recently been students think semiotics might be important, but other students whose formal studies are further behind them are confused about it
all. Eventually, it is suggested that Deirdre keep a list of problematic or
jargon terms. She quickly has occasion to add *metalinguistics* to her list.

Joanna is also concerned with group dynamics and thinks the groups
should be careful not to splinter the class. The students should all make a
point of supporting one another in this enterprise, she says. I suggest it
might be a good idea if someone reassured me once a week that the venture would not fall apart. Joanna smilingly wants to know if I intend to
get off the ship before it sinks. Guy remarks that this is a good South
African tradition.

Mavis remembers that her group has stressed the need to be critical—and to study the nature of criticality. This rouses Deirdre again, who
adds the word to her list. There is a short sharp discussion of the different
meanings of the word *critical* in various contexts.

Brandon wants to look at the hierarchy of constraints in schools, from
the government, material inadequacies, the use of materials written by
someone else, and the effects of television and of violence. He is also
concerned with the constraints imposed by teachers on themselves due
to their lack of knowledge or confidence.

Albert says his group is concerned about particular Soweto constraints, such as large class sizes. How can teachers teach language to
classes with seventy children and still get through to everyone? There are
also problems of inadequate professional training for teachers and their
lack of confidence.

Brandon asks about students who only encounter English at school—
maybe for only an hour a day in the English classroom. Standards of teaching English are falling, and history is again being taught in the vernacular.

Joanna says children hear English for only about an hour a day in
many rural schools. But many African children would prefer not to learn
in the vernacular. This rejection of one's own language, I am to learn, is
one of the most devastating consequences of colonial education.

Laura's group is in favour of visiting schools as a first step before asking questions about what should go into the course. The group particularly wants to look at three broad areas:

1. The general context of school and society; teachers (their backgrounds, training, relationships to students, competence in English, and attitudes towards teaching); pupils (their age and socioeconomic backgrounds); and the criteria for passing and failing
2. What is being taught
3. How it is being taught.

The group would like to investigate what exactly they already know and what they don't know.

Thomas's group has a final suggestion: they should observe other classes in their own schools, although that might require more diplomacy and tact than visiting other schools.

I AM CONCERNED THAT THE GROUPS seem to be concentrating on very general areas of study rather than on ways in which they might better understand the particular situations they are in. They are also getting into complex issues that go beyond relying on professors, checking in the library, or even conducting research. They are talking about factors that all teachers should be sensitive to: continuing considerations rather than gaps in knowledge that can be filled once and for all. These are mostly questions that I believe are never answered without specific knowledge of the particular individuals involved and of the situations they are in.

I must be patient about this at the end of only the first week of the course. The students may well have different points of view. But I hope they can go beyond the point of simply cataloguing questions that they would like someone to answer. The first step towards independent thinking in education at all levels must be to learn that you cannot depend on other people to solve your problems.

Chapter 5

Soweto

Soweto is like a huge polyp on the southwestern side of Johannesburg, attached to the city but not part of it. It began as a scattering of barrack-type hostels built to accommodate black workers brought in to labour in the mines. The workers came on contracts that did not provide for wives or families, and the hostels were intended to provide temporary segregated accommodation for solitary males. Some families came anyway, and others were established. Transients moved into hostels when men with families moved out, setting up communities that grew into townships and spread seamlessly and seemingly endlessly over featureless low hillsides. The townships also became areas to which other blacks were compulsorily removed to prevent them from living—but not working—in white residential areas, under the apartheid philosophy that the "races" were ordained to live "separate but equal."

Soweto is not even the name of a specific place. It is a linguistic barbarism—an ugly bureaucratic abbreviation for South Western Townships, a collection of twenty-six communities with individual names like Meadowlands and Orlando that have grown, multiplied, and merged into a metropolis larger than the city that conceived it. The number of people living in Soweto today is at least two million, possibly three. In the seething babel of Soweto, multilingualism thrives and language change is constant.

There are three ways to get to Soweto. With a car, you can drive along a freeway that takes you straight out of Johannesburg and into the townships. There are no back streets you can wander down between one and the other; road links have been deliberately constricted for ease of control. If you have no car, you can pack yourself into one of the thousands of "black taxis"—fast, overcrowded, and sometimes perilous minibuses that ply erratically between Soweto and the city. Among the few commercial enterprises so far established by black entrepreneurs, they take the place of bus services largely destroyed in the uprisings of the eighties. Or you can take the electric train—speedy, frequent, and in recent years the setting for gruesome, often random, and apparently senseless killings by black gang members. Passengers, even school children, have died because they failed to produce a particular political party membership card on demand.

Few black workers have cars, and those that do are not encouraged to bring them into the city and its white suburbs. Early every weekday morning, hundreds of thousands of cleaners, cooks, drivers, gardeners, labourers, domestic workers, and a few schoolchildren come into Johannesburg by black taxi or train, and every evening they all go home to Soweto again. (Similar journeys are made every day from the other great seething township of Alexandra, to the northwest of Johannesburg, and from lesser ghettoes elsewhere. Johannesburg stands in a litter of compounds created for the people it wanted to employ but not to live with.)

Soweto has its own suburbs and socioeconomic divisions. Many residents, including Nelson Mandela and Archbishop Desmond Tutu, live in neighbourhoods of tidy stucco villas that have been established for years. These districts of Soweto are visually indistinguishable from some of the developments of small houses in the older white areas of Johannesburg, except that Sowetan dwellings almost invariably shelter many more people than a white suburban house would be expected to contain. More recently, tracts of diminutive boxy brick houses have been developed in other parts of Soweto in an attempt to provide halfway decent homes for some of the population (and sometimes the potential of a return on white investment). But the majority of Sowetans live in grossly unsanitary and overcrowded conditions with little hope of improvement and a constant threat of violence and dispossession, an affront to any human being and a particularly obscene insult to people originally brought in solely to provide a more comfortable life for others.

Huge expanses of Soweto have no domestic water, no sewers, and no electricity. Garbage is not collected, and streets are not paved. There are no sidewalks, few trees, and no parks or other public spaces. There are no shopping centres, no banks, and no cinemas. Until recently, there were no legal commercial black enterprises at all. There was an official fiction that people did not *live* in the townships, but merely lodged in them temporarily while working in the city or in the mines. Nothing was permitted that might encourage people to stay, or at least to enjoy staying. These areas of Soweto are like a vast and temporary encampment.

Some areas—like many of the outlying "rural" townships—are little more than chaotic conglomerations of shacks made up of bits of wood, plastic, metal siding, sacking, or with luck some concrete blocks. Some are just lean-tos of junk. These areas look like communities that no one wants to bother with, which is what they are. The only exceptions seem to be people who actually live in the hovels, trying to lead decent lives in them, tending tiny parched gardens, hanging out laundry on lines shorter than a blanket, and sending tidy, laughing children off to school if it is safe and possible for them to go. (Several teachers told me that Soweto parents were more likely to buy or make school materials for their children than white parents were, who expected to have everything supplied.)

Much of the life of crowded Soweto takes place out of doors—alongside dusty roadsides lined with stalls, kitchens, and workshops and among wandering dogs, cats, chickens, goats, cows, donkeys, and horses (employed to transport wood and coal for primitive heating systems). When the threat of violence temporarily recedes, when there are no protests or demonstrations or funerals to attend, and when the security forces are not making a sweep, Soweto is a bustling colourful amalgam of urban and rural life.

THERE ARE NUMEROUS SCHOOLS IN SOWETO, though not enough. And many have been abandoned, especially high schools. Schools are usually easy to distinguish by their single-storey brick institutional appearance, the political graffiti on their walls, the high wire fences around them, their unkempt and unsurfaced grounds, and—especially—by the vast numbers of broken windows, damaged doors, and other signs of vandalism.

I could not believe that the first high school I visited in Soweto was functioning. It looked like a factory blasted by bombs. Every window was broken, doors hung from their hinges, walls had intruder-sized holes in them, all the ceilings were smashed in, and all the electrical fittings were ripped out. There were no toilet facilities, no food services, no library, and no laboratories. I counted twenty-six totally wrecked classrooms, all wide open to the elements—and then I saw 1,300 students and forty staff arrive to spend the working day in them.

The school might once have been a pleasant place, with an inside verandah around a treed courtyard. But the grass was now totally overgrown where it was not worn away, and all the walkways and the road in were rutted expanses of red dust (mud when it rained, of course). Because there was no protection, every classroom was deep in dust from the raw earth outside. Students had to sweep out every morning before classes could start, and the school could not even provide them with brooms.

There were no pictures or decorations on the bare brick walls, no cupboards, and no bookshelves. There were no books, except for the few that the teacher and students might bring in. There was no teacher's desk, battered tables were piled up in corners overnight, and orange plastic seats lay in heaps inside and out. The principal told me things were much better now than they used to be. Students did now come to school, and they didn't attack teachers as often. But the DET would not pay for repairs, security, or maintenance, and the parents had become tired of replacing windows that were immediately smashed again.

The principal's office was a hut barely large enough to accommodate a desk, chair, and filing cabinet, with one wall and the ceiling falling down, security bars where windows used to be, and a padlocked iron gate where the front door hung uselessly. The shack for the staff was worse: two old tables, four chairs, and a few cupboards for the forty teachers, with everything cluttered with exercise books waiting in the dust to be marked.

There was a history of violence in the school. Three days after the Soweto student protests began in 1976, an armoured police truck came onto the school yard. It was overturned and burned by students.

Before lessons could begin, a classroom had to be cleared of some older students and visitors who had taken possession to gamble and smoke *dagga* (marihuana). The teacher who did this, quietly and firmly, was the head of the English department, who had worked in the school for ten years. He was also a student in the Honours course of the Department of Applied English Language Studies at the University of the Witwatersrand, where he had been terrified by the entrance test. He was Albert.

THE DAY BEGAN, AS IT DID IN EVERY SOUTH AFRICAN SCHOOL, with thanks to God. The uniformed students lined up, sang hymns lustily, and listened to a homily. Some arrived late, but they were not questioned. Sixteen people had been killed in Soweto during the weekend. On a wall, there was a notice from the student union calling all matriculation students out later to attend a protest meeting.

I joined over forty standard 10 students (seventeen years old or over) packed into one room, sitting three or four to desks built for two and sharing one book (and sometimes one pencil) at each desk. Some of the battered wood and tubular steel desks lacked their seats, so students had to wedge chairs into them. The wind brought clouds of dust into every eye and throat. The first lesson of the morning was poetry.

The poem Albert had selected was *Pieta,* by South African Guy Butler. It is ostensibly about the death of Jesus, but Albert underlined the South African connotations. The poem begins "Tremendous, marching through smashed buildings. . . ." Like people in Soweto marching to the rallies, observed Albert. He held the attention of the class, though like me they had to strain to hear his faint voice.

Two students came in to take up a collection in a brown envelope for a student whose father had died. A few students found coins to contribute. Three female students came to me outside the class and appealed to me to help the school get books. They wanted to be educated, they said.

In another room, a group of standard 8 students (fifteen-year-olds) was dramatizing a poem called *The African Beggar*, acting the parts with gusto. This teacher was less explanatory and more interrogatory than Albert, using a study guide to provide a paraphrase of the poem. He spoke a discursive conversational black South African English, which I found difficult to understand. The students, like all South African students, raised their hands to be invited to respond. But they paid attention, and they laughed.

There was no equipment of any kind in the school, not even a telephone. When it rained, the classrooms were flooded. And the teachers said they had no hope of anything better. They were assigned to the school and could not go anywhere else. Albert admitted that he often thought of quitting, but what would happen to students if all the teachers left?

ALBERT LIVES IN ONE OF THE SMARTER PROFESSIONAL AREAS of Soweto, in a small, single-storey, stucco home on a tiny plot of land with his wife and a shifting population of relatives. His parents fled intertribal political violence in Natal to come to Johannesburg, where his father, a literate man, got a job in a mines office. But his father died when Albert was a child, and because of the "influx laws," his mother and the family had to move immediately back to Natal (where authorities said they "belonged," even though Albert was born in Soweto).

But his mother still could not tolerate the violence or the lack of opportunity or education there for her children and returned to Johannesburg. She did this by marrying a much older man who already had a wife and family elsewhere. Albert did well at school until the matriculation examination, which he failed in English. This would typically mean the end of education and of hopes for a career. He left school immediately with a friend, and they spent a year just reading anything in English they could find. They read mainly Dickens, popular among young Sowetans because he wrote about poor people they could identify with. As a result, Albert ended knowing more about Victorian London than he did about contemporary Africa. He also became an accomplished reader and writer of English, which enabled him to pass his matriculation examination and then to get a teaching diploma part-time at Soweto College of Education while working for two years in a Soweto bottle factory. While teaching, he studied evenings to get a B.A. from the University of South Africa (UNISA), which conducts only correspondence courses. He married a teacher from Natal whose family had also moved away because so many people were being killed there, including her young brother.

THE DET IS A HIGHLY STRUCTURED, top-down authoritarian educational system. There are two tests every year to determine if students should be promoted, and there is a continual preoccupation with marks. Teachers labour through a syllabus that specifies in minute detail what must be taught in each thirty-five-minute period, working towards tests that they know their students will not understand. Many teachers try to subvert the system, especially when they have the support of their principal or some of their colleagues. They believe that children are more literate than their examinations show them to be and that teachers are more competent than the curriculum allows them to be.

In most DET schools, children are taught in their mother tongue or another vernacular language for four years, with English or Afrikaans as a subject. English is usually introduced as a medium of instruction in standard 3, the equivalent of grade 5 in North America. In South African schools, the first two years (starting at age five or six) are called grade 1 and grade 2 (or sometimes grade sub A and grade sub B), followed by standard 1 (the equivalent of North American grade 3), standard 2 (the equivalent of North American grade 4), and so forth.

Black children are frequently moved into a language they do not understand before they have had very much experience thinking and learning in a language with which they are familiar. They are regarded as functionally literate if they have 700-word English vocabularies, although they are expected to read materials demanding knowledge of 7,000 words or more. And there is a lack of skilled teachers, many of whom do not come from literate backgrounds. Many children, especially from ambitious families, may be discouraged from using their mother tongue.

An extensive investigation of the traumatic effects of the "language switch" is contained in six volumes of *Threshhold Reports* by Carol Macdonald, published by the Human Sciences Research Council in Pretoria. A more accessible summary of the report has been published by Macdonald and Burroughs (1991). The authors tell of children bewildered by the urban, technological culture of schools. Even if the children did everything expected of them, English as a subject in the first four years would not provide them with a strong enough foundation for using English to learn ten subjects on the first day of the fifth year.

Children were expected to move into the English medium, understanding technical and scientific terms, after a total of 350 hours of experience of English (equivalent to about a month in real life). They jumped from the simple stories of English readers at the end of standard 2 to geography, history, and general science texts at the beginning of standard 3. Learning tasks became essentially nonsense to them. There were often dramatic changes in teaching style in standard 3, partly due to the teachers' lack of confidence in English. The teachers often became authoritarian—"talk and chalk"—in contrast to their "motherly" role in junior primary classes. Students became passive recipients of information, learning by rote. They could not discuss.

Questions usually tested children's memory, not their understanding.

Many teachers had come through DET systems and experienced only "rote-rhythm" methods of drumming facts into learners, who were expected to learn by chanting responses to teachers' questions. Teachers were·expected to teach in a language that they knew would not be effective. There were also problems of large classes and lack of materials.

School came as a shock for children from "traditional" nonformal systems, and they could not cope. "The traditional African way of teaching is based on different ideas. Learning happens in an informal way, where children learn to do tasks by observing and then trying to do what they have seen" (Macdonald & Burroughs, 1991). The authors urge that this mode of teaching and learning be taken into account and built on. Schools were not sensitive to children's needs, and children dropped out or stayed away. It was estimated that at least two million children were not currently in school.

Macdonald and Burroughs note:

> Almost one in four African children who enters grade one does not reach grade two the following year; half of all African children do not graduate from primary school in the minimum seven year period. . . . it is estimated that, apart from those who do not attend school at all, the system produces one third of a million illiterate children. (Foreword)

Other observations by Macdonald and Burroughs include the following: Children's thinking develops most quickly and easily in their first language (p. 31). Second language builds on first language (p. 32). Children whose mother tongue is not English need special provisions to achieve as well as mother tongue speakers of English do; otherwise, there is no equality of opportunity (p. 37). Preschool experience is most important, especially in nonliterate societies. Children with some knowledge of books and stories are better prepared than children who have no knowledge of books (p. 43).

The straight-for-English alternative from the beginning of school had been adopted in the Southern Africa country of Zambia, and children still could not use English outside after nine years. Children did much better if they first become literate in their own language, but they still needed highly competent teachers because they required lots of support in English.

Macdonald and Burroughs recommended that children start in their own language, which would help their thinking and ability to learn and use other languages, but they acknowledged this was a delicate issue for most South Africans because first-language education had been associated with apartheid. But the swing in other African countries was to giving full teaching status to national languages. They also recommended a South African curriculum in place of the current Eurocentric one (p. 61) and a "teacher-guided discovery approach for learners" (p. 64) that was relevant to children's lives.

IN THE SECOND-YEAR CLASS AT WITS, I discussed the inseparability of learning and language. In the tutorial that followed, we talked about how children learn conventions we never think we are taught, such as how long to hold eye contact, how to gesture, and how long to wait before interrupting. A black student asked why whites smiled at blacks in an odd way, as if they had to force themselves to do so. No one else had noticed this, but there was no wish to dispute the assertion. The student then told how a university official was abrupt with him on the telephone because, the student thought, the official could tell from his voice that he was black. He wanted to know if I thought the official was rude. I fudged: Different things were rude in different cultures, and some officials seemed to be rude all the time. This did not satisfy the student, who demanded my personal opinion on whether that particular official had been rude to him as a black on that particular occasion. Other black students came to my rescue while white students looked on. A woman said the official was probably busy and perhaps didn't understand what the student was saying. A young man said they should keep the discussion general, not personal. Another said that black-white issues should be kept out of the discussion. A white student muttered, "Some hope."

Outside the room afterwards, I rather tentatively told the complaining student that he should not have called on me publicly to support his own point of view. He surprised me with a spirited nod of agreement and a knowing grin. We parted with the "solidarity handshake," alternately grasping the other's right thumb with the right hand, yet another kind of language.

THE FAILURE RATE ON THE DEPARTMENT'S ESL COURSE the previous year had been 20 per cent, which was considered good. The department had planned on 25 per cent. But of course, the cutoff point was arbitrary. There was no objective measure of what ought to be considered a pass or a failure in this course. The actual failure rate on examinations was much higher—between 30 per cent and 40 per cent—but the marks allocated for term work pulled many students up. The "discrepancy" between course marks and examination marks bothered some professors from other departments, who suspected the staff might be "marking leniently" to help students get through. On the other hand, course marks might have been a better indicator of student ability without the time pressure of examinations.

The 200 pages of handouts that ESL students received (and paid for) were mainly exercises or descriptions of English grammar on which they were tested. The book lists for the course also focused on English grammar and sentence analysis; the staff said black students were more likely to buy books than white students were. The course also included workshops on writing, concentrating on "academic" paragraphs and short essays, with exercises every week, all of which were marked by staff.

The staff tended to be uncompromising in the face of reports of studies elsewhere that showed no difference between non-English-mother-tongue students who received special academic preparation before taking courses taught in English and others who did not. A research review from Fiji documented evidence that independent reading in English was more effective than specific instruction in the language (Elley, 1991). A study in India even indicated that the specific teaching of English grammar interfered with the learning of English grammar (Prabhu, 1987).

PRESIDENT DE KLERK ANNOUNCED the wording of the referendum question: basically, whether the white electorate was in favour of the manner in which he was conducting the negotiations at Codesa.

The next morning, the leader of the white right-wing extremists told a meeting of his "black shirts" and their applauding supporters that his party, the African Resistance Party (AWB), would participate in the referendum after all, despite an earlier decision to boycott it. They would probably not sway the vote, but they would avoid being isolated and could possibly gain a lot of conservative support and even—in their imaginations—come eventually to lead the opposition to the government. The AWB policy was for separate self-governing Afrikaner territories in South Africa.

There was a competing interest. South Africa had been accepted again into international sport, and its cricket team, hurriedly sponsored by a cigarette manufacturing company, was playing in Australia for the first time in over thirty years. Headlines and continuous television coverage trumpeted a great surge of national pride and hope. The country would demonstrate that it had not been damaged by international isolation and that its athletes could still beat the best of the rest of the world.

Chapter 6

Week Two

MONDAY

Only a few students arrive this afternoon. Faith (who doesn't stay long because she must go to her part-time job at the library), Charles (who comes eagerly to everything, with long position papers he has prepared the night before), Laura (always cool and level-headed, but she says she finds the course approach "exciting"), Benjamin (businesslike after his drive from Bophuthatswana), and Deirdre (who usually comes in late, trailing anxieties with her). Deirdre still doesn't know what the course is about. She says she expected simply to be told what she was supposed to know. She wouldn't treat her own students in that way, but it was a surprise when the university behaved differently. Deirdre, like Joanna, comes out with unpredictable observations or questions that are disturbing if not discouraging. But she is diffident rather than challenging: "I hate to ask this stupid question, but. . . ."

I have inaugurated a small, informal Monday lunchtime brown-bag meeting for students, staff, and visitors—anyone who wants to come. Just an opportunity to talk, without even a formal title. It is attended by a few staff members—usually very vocal—and by a few students—usually very quiet, though today they are joined by Joanna, as alert and challenging as ever. I mentioned my concern with the possible *costs* of massive efforts to teach English: the cost to other languages in South Africa (which many parents and children seem not particularly to care about) and the cost to the children who fail to learn English under mandatory conditions. A colleague thought that our job was to see that "every child had access to English" and that the way we did it was no different from any other language-teaching department. Some departments are concerned with the teaching of Russian. Ours is concerned with the teaching of English. And that is that. This was Joanna's view as well. But I think there is a difference: Russian is not compulsory in South Africa; English is.

Requiring every child to learn English from an early age as part of the official curriculum and even as national policy will not guarantee that every child learns English. In fact, it is a poor educational tactic because it catches many children at an inappropriate time in their lives, when many teachers are inadequate to the task. It guarantees that many children acquire the label of failure who would not otherwise do so. I'm not a failure in learning to speak Russian because I've never tried. I would be a failure if Russian had been on the curriculum and I hadn't learned.

I also question whether increasing the numbers of black students who are fluent in English will empower them. Many people in South Africa and elsewhere are literate and competent in English, yet they have little power. On the other hand, South Africans who become active politically or who have a job seem able to acquire adequate English competence for their needs without difficulty.

In the Honours class, we talk about the possibility of studying how students who do speak "good English" actually learned to do so and about the consequences of failing to learn the language when it is on the curriculum.

Laura claims she learned to speak Afrikaans at her all-white English language girls' school without difficulty. All the other students at the school did the same. But afterwards, she admits that few of them would have been able to move into an all-Afrikaans-speaking university and cope with their studies—at least not for a year. And she is still unable to understand television programmes in Afrikaans. I ask her why, then, she thinks that she learned to speak Afrikaans at school. She says she passed the examinations.

Faith has excellent English. She says she learned it as a child in an all English-speaking school with no difficulty. She gives a lot of credit to her parents, who expected their children to work hard at their studies and to succeed. But Faith has little recollection of how her learning actually took place.

Benjamin thinks he learned English at school—it wasn't spoken anywhere else—but over a long period. He read a lot and was always motivated to learn English, as he thought many black students were. They believe it will help them in careers. There was no resistance to English in black schools, although many students died in protests against the imposition of Afrikaans.

Laura, who teaches children from the sprawling and violent black township of Alexandra, wonders what might motivate small children to devote so much effort to learning a language that has no current relevance in their lives.

The students persist in referring to the mandatory all-English class-room situation after standard 3 (age ten) as immersion. I try to point out what I see as an obvious difference between exclusively English language instruction in South Africa and, for example, the usual immersion situation in Canada. Under Canadian immersion, the main effort is always to ensure that students understand the target language, in which the teachers are fluent. When someone says "Fermez la porte, s'il vous plaît," the door is indicated. But with all-English instruction in black South African classrooms, the situation for many students much of the time is total incomprehension.

TUESDAY

I drop in on the morning group for half an hour. They are having an ardent session about the use of tape recorders in classroom research. The instructor likes them because they provide "data" that the teacher can reflect on to study communication. The students are less enthusiastic, thinking the technology changes the nature of the communication and also that it misses important things that should receive attention (such as what teachers and students are doing when they talk and how they feel).

They also discuss independent reading. Eleanor and Deirdre both say there is extensive time for free reading in their own schools, with no set materials and everyone expected just to read. This doesn't sound like anyone else's actual experience of South African schools. Charles thinks a particular kind of principal is required for any free reading to take place. He says the practice is in direct opposition to the official curriculum view, which stresses standardization and common activities.

Elizabeth talks movingly of the situation in her Soweto school. There has been violence again: This time, two people were killed directly outside the school, and students had to walk past their bodies. The school was upset, and she has been encouraging students to keep diaries of their feelings, which they can share with her (though she does not mark them). They also write poetry, for example on the topic of respect. When she asks students to write poetry, she writes with them under the same conditions, sharing what she produces. The students are very critical of her, she says. They tell her that her rhymes are terrible. I am told that Elizabeth is very unusual for a black teacher. I ask her where she learned to teach the way she does; she says she follows her feelings.

Joanna has been eager to talk with me. She thinks my comment yesterday that learning English does not guarantee that anyone will become empowered was glib. She seems to think I don't believe people should be given the opportunity to learn English, which was certainly not my point. She disagrees with my assertion that there is no guarantee that anyone who learns English will automatically share in the power and wealth of the country. Because English is the language of power, people who have access to English will have access to power, she says. I point out that many of the South African political leaders who were jailed in the past thirty years spoke excellent English.

Of course, all other things being equal, I can see that it is probably better to be fluent in English than not to be. But I suspect that many people who have not learned English have not lost very much (provided they haven't been stigmatized in school) and that many people who *need* English, from waiters and bus drivers to politicians and business executives, have learned enough of it without the language being a compulsory part of their formal education. But I must be careful about raising such arguments in South Africa. They provoke highly emotional responses.

A PROBLEM FOR STUDENTS IN THE HONOURS COURSE, according to Laura, is that they are not used to being asked to make decisions, or to learn in situations where what they expect to learn is not delivered to them.

WEDNESDAY

Most of the students show up punctually for the afternoon general session. I take a seat on the side, between Brandon and Elizabeth, and quietly propose to Brandon that they begin by selecting a chairperson from among themselves just to keep the session moving. Brandon follows this suggestion and finds himself appointed. He takes the role serenely, moving to the solitary desk by the chalkboard and writing an "agenda" on the board. The first item is the rather mysterious word "newsprint," which Mavis is anxious to put at the head of the list, followed by items on school visits, observations of classrooms in their own schools, the identification of issues, and something called Charles's proposal. Nothing comes of any of this because Mavis's newsprint item dominates the rest of the session.

Tentatively, Mavis unravels a roll of sheets of newsprint, each cut to broadsheet newspaper size. There are sheets for each of the previous week's groups. She puts three of the sheets on the board with tape—obliterating Brandon's agenda—with the headings:

Reading, writing, talking, and listening
Role of grammar, syntax, semantics, and phonology
Evaluation/assessment/teaching.

With her audience's full attention, Mavis's confidence grows and she moves into a demonstrator mode. She says that what is on each sheet could be the basis of a "planned approach" to what the groups are trying to do. They show how groups can "attack," modify, or expand on topics.

On each of the three sheets on the board, she has listed the "resources" each group has available (based on the four categories I set out at the first session, which I thought had been totally ignored): the group's experience, observations, reading, and other people. Beneath the resources, she has put the heading "questions" (for what the group wants to know on each topic, she explains) and the heading "action" (for what should be done to find answers—where they would go, what they would do, and whom they would invite). All of this could be modified, but it is a basis for action, a way perhaps for small groups to get to work. She smiles hopefully.

Joanna responds vigorously. She challenges the meaning of terms, as if Mavis, having made the presentation, is responsible for defending every aspect of it. Joanna sees a problem with headings at this time: They gave closure (which others dispute) and direction (which others think a good thing).

Deirdre, always anxious to curtail contentious debate, wants to begin inviting the academic staff to talk on some of the topics that have been listed. Charles thinks they are missing a step. The suggestions should first be prioritized.

Mavis, regaining control, says that all of her pieces of newsprint should first be displayed and starts unravelling more. Laura says she likes a beginning focus even if later it has to be abandoned.

Brandon, trying to get back to his agenda, wants to know if the group is now "identifying the issues."

Joanna now thinks there is probably a lot of overlap in the small-group suggestions. She brings out four pages of summaries of her own—a kind of complement to Mavis's work—and starts to read from them: another list of headings. I leave the room to make copies of Joanna's summaries for the group. I am delighted that the groups seem to have been so active and productive. Unfortunately, I have some trouble with the photocopying machine and have to return without the copies. When I get back, it doesn't matter.

The walls are festooned with sheets of Mavis's newsprint, one for each of the "major topics" that the small groups have defined. But to my dismay, Alice is putting on the board what I have not wanted to see as an early topic of conversation: an outline of the previous year's programme. Apparently, the class had wanted to know what had been done last year, and Alice obliged, with all the topic headings, the number of quarters spent on each one, and the names of the lecturers. The list comprises the following topics:

Syntax
Phonetics
First-language acquisition
Second-language acquisition
Sociology
Discourse analysis
Language policy and planning
Methodology and testing.

While acknowledging the artificiality of the categories, Alice and her colleague Marina begin discussing which ones they had found "fascinating," "topical," "a waste of time," and "useful but should be condensed." They start a discussion of which lecturers should perhaps be invited back to talk to the entire class. There is also a good deal of erasing and rewriting as topics and subtopics are moved around on the board to try to get them to fit together in satisfying ways. I feel that everything is getting out of hand, with the approach to how an Honours course should be designed starting from the wrong direction: trying to structure a collection of academic topics without consideration of what the course as a whole should try to achieve. I manage to stay silent, and an ally comes on the scene.

Brandon also thinks matters are getting out of control, and he asks how they can bring all of this—waving his hand around the walls and across the board—together.

But Mavis, always looking for structure to hold on to, asks Alice how she would organize the course this year. Alice says she would throw out first-language acquisition, which she thinks had been a waste of time since they were concerned with second-language learning. She would also "scale down" phonetics from two quarters to three or four lectures and "cut syntax some."

Marina offers a note of caution to Alice: "We should be careful what we say. We've never taught in school. Surely the point of our going into schools now is to answer the kinds of questions you're asking."

I suggest that it is premature even to think about "answers." The point of the discussions, the research, and the school visits was to decide what the questions should be and how the rest of the course might go about examining them, students and instructors together. I doubt whether staff could know all the answers to student questions—especially questions that students had not yet thought of asking. But an intense discussion begins about which particular instructors might be invited to talk about the headings on the board. Joanna surprises me by suggesting they might find it useful to ask my opinion on some topics, as one of the resources.

Charles appeals for them not to get tied to the topic headings on the board: "Let's postpone all this; we just keep switching around."

Laura likes the idea of moving into small groups again to work on topics of particular interest. Marina now wants to "prioritize." Alice thinks they will be in trouble if they do not make a decision on whether the course should aim at producing better teachers or at providing a variety of theoretical insights. I go back to my office to make some phone calls.

When I return, Joanna is at the chalkboard, putting up what I can only describe as a spider or perhaps a spider's web. There is an unidentified circle in the middle with lines radiating out to such labels as:

Skills
Materials
Multiculturalism
Bilingualism
Discourse analysis
Language acquisition
Cognition
Role of grammar and error
ESL/EFL (some lively discussion here until Laura elicits the fact that
    although ESL means English as a second language, EFL does not mean
    English as a first language but English as a foreign language)
Interference theory
Contextual constraints
The politics of educational control
Language policy
Evaluation
Intelligence
Semiotics
Social factors.

Once again, there is a good deal of rubbing out, rewording, and moving of items around on the board, together with suggestions about who might be invited in to talk on particular topics.

Albert at last wonders aloud whether he is alone or whether others think as he does that they are rushing to decide what they should do without considering why they should do it. Mavis now makes an appeal to prioritize topics and to divide them into groups.

I contemplate giving an impromptu lecture on the uselessness of slogans and labels and on the ugliness of terms like prioritize. Instead, I comment as neutrally as I can that there would be no shortage of instructors ready to give entire series of talks on any of the topics listed on the board but that that would not resolve any of the students' problems. Instead of inviting someone to come in to talk about multiculturalism, for example, they might consider themselves exploring and discussing why multiculturalism might be an important topic and in what way.

I also get a little more directive than I had intended and suggest that they use Tuesday afternoons for strategy sessions like the one they have just been having but that the Thursday sessions should be devoted to working groups getting on with particular matters rather than wandering all over the globe.

But there is no need or opportunity for me to pursue the matter further. There seems to be a sudden general awareness that the afternoon is almost over, and small conversations break out about what the next move should be. I choose that moment to leave—or to start to leave.

On my way out, I am challenged by Mavis, who wants "materials development" to be included in the course. I ask how she has reached that decision when the students have not even considered what they want materials to do or even whether materials are needed. She says that teachers have to have something for practical classroom reasons. Again, I question why the development of materials should automatically be a concern. The world is already full of materials, more than teachers can handle. Teachers can teach reading with newspapers and magazines. Perhaps they should. These are the kinds of matters that should be considered first, not how to produce more materials. Mavis is dubious. She doesn't see how teachers can teach without materials.

Vicky and Marina tell me they would be interested in a lecture on Vygotsky. When I ask why, Alice says lots of instructors seem to think that Vygotsky is important. I suggest that instead of a lecture on Vygotsky for all of them, which would take up at least an afternoon, one or two of them might go into the library and browse through books by or about Vygotsky for an hour or two, by which time they might have a pretty good idea of what Vygotsky has to offer and of how much time should be spent on him.

I rashly say that Vygotsky's contribution, though important, could be summarized in a couple of sentences. The rest is argument, evidence, and applications, which the class as a whole might well do without, even though such matters could be pursued and examined by one or two of them. Of course, I am immediately challenged to summarize Vygotsky's position in a couple of sentences. I say that anything a child can do with help today, the child will be able to do alone tomorrow. There is, therefore, no point in teaching anything that a child does not immediately understand and find useful or relevant. Alice and Marina say they would

like to give Vygotsky more study. In the next few weeks, they and
Thomas will do some extensive reading.

THURSDAY

I expect a general session to "discuss strategy," but once again the class
surprises me. They go into their smaller groups and start work immediately. Also to my surprise, I discover that many of them arrived and made
their decisions early: ten minutes before the class was due to begin.

Joanna has some questions for me about "whole language." She
wants to know exactly how this approach to literacy teaching looks in
the classroom. I say that whole language is not a methodology but a
resistance movement against commercial programs, standardised curricula and tests, and meaningless materials. It is supportive of teachers,
"real books," reading to children, independent reading, assisted writing,
encouragement, and publication. Joanna is in a receptive mood; she says
this helps. Then she brings up again my comments that deciding to teach
all children English would not necessarily empower them and might
have a cost. She reiterates that not to teach English would deny children
access to the power that the English language gives. Several of my colleagues have also in their own ways told me the same. They say I do not
understand the political situation in South Africa and should not make
such statements. I try a final time to spell out exactly what I mean, but
Joanna accuses me of not listening to her. I do not see that I can try again
in South Africa

ANOTHER STAFF MEMBER COMES IN and joins a group, loudly asserting the
importance of certain topics on the Honours curriculum. I divert the colleague into an adjacent room, and we discuss the role of staff at these
meetings. The colleague thinks the staff have a responsibility to guide
students, who cannot be left to their own initiative, to "flounder about."

The domination of students by staff members has been a growing
concern for me, and I have seen it intimidate some students. The original
idea was that students and staff should work together, but staff members
dominate any group they join. It is not totally their fault: Students automatically look to the academic staff for approval and for the initiation of
new directions. They did it to me, though they are beginning not to. But
the problem is worse for my colleagues; they have something to lose.

I raise this issue with the students. Some stay silent, but others say
they cannot talk with staff the way they talk with one another or with me.
They know the staff will at some point be evaluating them. In any case,
the staff are "authorities"; it is not appropriate for students to dispute with

them what should be in the course. The students also feel they cannot isolate themselves from the staff. They do not want "bad feelings." (It is different with me; I am an outsider who does not identify with the administration. I have opinions that I am not reluctant to offer, but these have the same status as student opinions, which I am anxious to hear. I am accepted in the groups, and my continual note taking is not questioned.)

A decision is reached. The students will usually meet and work independently of the staff, who should only join specific groups by invitation at particular times. The staff have had at least a year to plan the Honours course without pressure from students; the students will now have six weeks to work on their recommendations without pressure from the staff. Then the "collaboration" can resume, when students and staff come together to share their views.

The decision is made, of course, without the involvement of the staff. I say I think I can explain it to them, and I try. I do not discern that there is immediate resentment and suspicion that will expand and burst upon me with great intensity at the end of the seven weeks.

THE COGNITION GROUP OF SECOND-YEAR STUDENTS has taken to meeting apart from the others, at a corner table or in a neighbouring room. Alice comes in and asks me about some questions they have formulated. The first is: "What is the relation between language and cognition?" This sounds to me like just another label, and I start to take it apart: "You can't ask a question like this. . . . " (Marina interposes: "I told you he'd say that.") "Why do you want to ask the question?" "Other people seem to think it is important," says Alice. "What does the question mean?" "We don't know." "So why ask it?"

I say that cognition is just a fancy word for thinking and that thinking takes place all the time. Language and thinking are inseparable. The educational problem is not the abstract issue of how language and thinking might be connected psychologically, physiologically, or philosophically (although specialists in each of these areas have conflicting points of view) but how language is used and thinking is encouraged in school. There is no language without thinking, and all human thinking involves language. (Even when we think about music or sport or love, we use language. Humans seem to have a compulsion to organize their world through language). We go on to a discussion about Whorf and the interactions among language, thinking, and culture. I give another minilecture, something I try but find very difficult to avoid. This is the staff-student problem again.

A similar thing happens when a question about "the relationship between first- and second-language acquisition" is asked. I ask, "Why use the jargon word *acquisition* rather than learning?" "It's the term that is used," I am told. "What does it mean?" "We don't know." There is a long discussion about Krashen's theories of language acquisition, about different uses of the word acquisition, and once more about metalanguage. Alice wants to know what metalanguage is. I explain that metalanguage is language about language and argue that common words should be used wherever possible. Everyone knows what the word *learning* means.

Responses like these do not satisfy the students. They seem to prefer to use abstruse terms and phrases even though they don't understand them. They find the jargon more compelling than real-life situations. They want to know about relationships among abstractions—as though some kind of algebraic formula will throw light on the way people think and learn—although I doubt this is the way they talk in their lives outside the university.

All the groups are now becoming intensely active. There is no problem with getting the students motivated or finding some *work* for them to do. They are all reading, writing, and participating in group discussions, though Eleanor, Bonnie, and Lucas appear reluctant to speak out in the class as a whole. But that is a matter of personality, not of failure to participate. They are *engaged.*

I go back to the small group with Brandon, Albert, Elizabeth, Gertrude, and anxious Mavis, who still wants to discuss materials. We talk a little about the distinction between the production of materials because teachers need them at a particular time in the classroom and the multimillion-dollar business and politics of materials publication. There is an understanding of this. We also have a discussion about intelligence, another matter clearly of importance to the group. I suggest that the educational problem is not one of capacity—which it is usually made out to be—but of *time.* Everyone needs more time than others to learn certain things people do. The problem in schools is that there is often not enough time for teachers or for many students to do what is expected to be done. If there were more time, there would be fewer failures. The same applies in the university.

Another question comes up that will be asked time and time again: Why teach grammar? My view is that no one ever learned language from grammar. People don't understand the grammar of a language until they've learned the language, and even then the explicit understanding is often minimal. Albert proposes that grammar is needed to pass exams, because exams are based on grammar. Instruction is always directed toward the exams, exams focus on the instruction, and it all has to be measurable and "markable"—things like vocabulary and grammar. He refers to Laura's story again; she thought she had learned Afrikaans in school because she had passed the examination. Grammar becomes a separate subject unrelated to language learning (just as I argue that phonics becomes a subject independent from reading).

The group comprising Laura, Faith, Charles, and Eleanor raises the question of time again, but in connection with the work of the Honours class itself. Charles had already broached it in a different context. They wonder if anyone is getting anywhere with all the questions that keep coming up, only to become fragmented into more complex questions. Charles suggests that the result will be a better set of questions. These could be the basis for the new course—not a random collection of topics to be covered, but a set of specific questions to be examined systematically by staff and students alike.

This is the first notion of what the outcome of the seven-week enterprise and the outline of the course might actually be like. For the first time, I feel we might get a significant result out of the sessions, not because everyone will become suddenly focused and single-minded but because the "questions" approach will be sufficiently self-organizing and challenging.

Chapter 7

Contrasts

One school in Soweto had all its windows intact. It was in the same township as Albert's high school, though in a slightly more prosperous residential area. In the modest gardens of the modest houses, children were playing. It was an oppressively hot afternoon in the parched height of summer, and any breeze raised clouds of ochre dust. When the children saw a party of four whites arrive, they strutted and flaunted their English. "Hello." "How are you?" "Where did you get that car?" They laughed as we stood in the street outside the gate in the high wire-mesh fence around the school, topped by coils of spiked wire (Soweto has its walls, too). Like the children, we were locked out.

The DET had followed its policy of strict ethnic segregation and had built the school solely for children speaking the Tswana language, who numbered about 200 in the district. In accordance with current policy, the students would be taught in Tswana—with English as a subject—for their first four years in school and would then continue with all-English instruction no matter how well they understood the language. About 500 children in the district who spoke other languages would receive no primary education (education was not compulsory for black children) or would have to try to find it further away—either by walking across the railroad tracks or by taking black taxis.

Led by the community's education committee, the parents were boycotting the school until it would accept *all* the children. They were trying to establish a school that ignored ethnic distinctions, which they regarded as part of the divisive heritage of apartheid. They wanted a school that would be "multilanguage." The result need not pose a problem for instruction. Soweto is a polyglot community, and most teachers and many children speak several African languages.

But the parents also wanted just one language of instruction—English—at all levels, from the children's first day in school. For them, as for many black Africans, the English language was a talisman for freedom, equality, and success. The DET had been adamant that only Tswana-speaking children should attend, so the school stayed closed.

The community faced other problems. Teachers competent in teaching English—or even in using the language themselves—were not easy to find in the DET system. The community had plans to find some books in English and to organize some teacher training to take care of this. They seemed to think that as soon as they had textbooks, teaching could begin in English.

They had fifteen teachers so far, taken from other schools in Soweto, who in accordance with current DET policy had not been replaced. (Replacements, supplies, and repairs were frequently withheld because the times were "transitional," the excuse for a great deal of delay and inaction within and outside government.) The teachers themselves were vacillating on the language issue because they did not want to upset the DET. Teaching jobs were not easy to find. But the parents and the community could be ruthless in their determination.

At the community meeting, the leader of the Soweto education committee delegation (a teacher elsewhere, who wore a business suit and tie despite the heat) wondered aloud if new teachers would be more flexible than experienced teachers in following community policies. The committee would fire teachers not in the preferred classification.

Communications were obviously inadequate. Some parents had heard that the DET had relaxed its restrictions and would allow four or even seven languages in the school, though not English alone. The education committee representative did not agree. One of the visitors said that a law had been passed the previous year that permitted *any* language medium of instruction in a school that the majority of parents wanted. But when parents wanted English, the DET authorities (who were mainly Afrikaners) were not ready to implement the law, partly because of the expense of providing English language materials. The representative suggested an "experimental" approach that the DET might accept and that would also be easier for the teachers and students. He outlined a scheme for employing increasing amounts of English over a three-year period, with liberal amounts of other languages as well.

It was suggested that the community "take advantage of gains" and reopen the school immediately, helping children to learn to read and write in their own languages. The local people seemed ready to listen, but the education committee man was determined that there should be no compromise. Many generations of black children had already been lost, he said. They would sacrifice another to get what they wanted in education.

TWO SOWETO SCHOOLS WHERE WITS HONOURS STUDENTS TAUGHT were temporarily closed over a dispute between teachers and the DET. At one school, the teachers were on strike. At the other, the students walked out because the teachers were not on strike.

THERE WAS ANOTHER DET SCHOOL on the outskirts of Soweto that had most of its windows intact, in a charming setting of neatly trimmed lawns and flower beds. This was because it was located in an army base and troops were available for security and gardening. The school itself was an old army barracks in reasonable condition. A few interior walls had been kicked in, but they could not be seen from the outside. But the rooms had been designed to be offices rather than school rooms, so they were all cramped and crowded.

Nevertheless, the school had 260 fee-paying students aged from six to sixteen and had turned away over 500 other applicants. "Safe" schools were not easy to find in Soweto. Half the children were from the families of black base personnel, and the other half were mostly from "middle-class" black families—teachers, lawyers, and postmen—who could afford the fees. It was regarded as a good, progressive school, and English was used as a primary language of instruction from the beginning.

At the outdoor assembly, the students in their neat school uniforms lined up under the trees facing the teachers and sang an upbeat Zulu hymn with deep harmonies and rhythmic movement. Then a teacher read a sermon on the theme of pride and boasting. She told the students they should never brag about what they would be when they left school—about being lawyers, engineers, or doctors. "God will decide what you will be," she said, "and your lives are just puffs of smoke. So stop this boastful talk." I asked the teacher later if that was an appropriate message for children being educated to take a leading role in the new South Africa, and she said it was what the materials issued by the DET said she had to say. Presumably, black children all over South Africa were told the same.

I sat in on an English class for the oldest students, with over forty students barely fitting into the room. There were a few small maps or diagrams on the wall and a few very used books. The students had performed badly on a test the previous day, and the teacher had called in the principal for a pep talk. The principal was a dynamo. He said he had only come in for five minutes to find out what was wrong, and he spent twenty minutes telling the students what it was. A female student knew the answer the moment he put the question to her: "Laxity." They didn't work hard enough at home, said the principal. They didn't read enough English or write enough English or hear enough English. Did they have library cards? Did they use them? He wasn't threatening them because he had never beaten them—and if he did beat them he would kill them—so they had better take his advice and read lots of English. In the course of his controlled tirade, he addressed all the students in the class individually to ask what they did in the evening instead of studying, threatening to call on their mothers to find out. The usual response was a bowed head. The students should read *The Adventures of Tom Sawyer,* he continued. That was a wonderful book—and he repeated the title. He told them to watch educational television, to write, and to take notes.

The principal noticed me trying to efface myself behind some students and recruited my assistance. I said reading was important in language learning. He leapt on this and asked me to tell the students what exactly they had to do. He instructed the teacher to write the "five points" I had mentioned on the board (actually there were only four), and he told the students to write down the five points, to memorize the five points, and to make the five points a class slogan.

Then it was the teacher's turn for embarrassment. I had said the students should read what interested them, and the principal said that was right. His own daughter wanted to read only about sex, but that was natural and he encouraged her; if the students wanted to read only about sex, that was all right by him. The teacher, a pious woman, obviously began to wish she had never invited the principal into her room. She protested that there was no language in sex. Principal: "There is if you read about it." Principal to students: "Read what you like." Teacher: "Not in my classroom." She began to say that she had some other materials for the students to read, but the principal said that at their age, the students were interested only in sex and she wouldn't be able to stop it. She said that she didn't see that it had to be sanctioned but that she would talk to the students after the principal had left.

After the principal had gone, the teacher resumed her reading lesson, with each student taking a turn to read from one book while forty others sat and listened (if they could hear—the students and most teachers spoke very softly) and waited in case they had to answer a question.

In their writing books, the students had copied definitions and examples of different kinds of English sentences. The student next to me had many of them wrong: Line after line, the teacher had put a line in red ink through her answers, with no explanation of what the error or correct response might be. But the teacher's final comment was "30/60—good work!" The typical pattern of the English textbook was a half-page passage (the first was from Shakespeare) followed by about five pages of smaller-type questions and exercises.

I went to the sub A class of five- and six-year-olds who had been in school only three months. The children, who had probably never heard English in their lives before, had been suddenly thrown into a world where not only was everything new but also in English. The exception was one lesson a day in "vernac"—either Zulu or Sotho—which may or may not have been their mother tongue. But the vernacular was a subject that they "studied"; they had to learn reading, writing, and math from the first day in the foreign language of English. And there was just one teacher with fifty-six students.

The school did not have a room big enough for fifty-six children, so they were seated in adjacent rooms with a wall between them. The teacher had managed to jam twenty-eight desks into each room, but there was no free space for the children to move in. They had to climb into their places over the desks of other students, and when there, they were stuck. The teacher could not get into the rooms, either. She had to teach the two rooms simultaneously by walking up and down the verandah outside and talking to the children through open doors and windows. She would write a task on one blackboard on the verandah, such as:

$$1 + \square = 2$$
$$1 + \square = 3$$
$$1 + \square = 4$$

She would then leave that group of children to copy it and work out what should be in the squares while she went to the other blackboard and wrote the identical task for the second group. Then she would go back and "mark" the work of the first group, helping children who were having difficulties (if they could reach over their desks to pass their books forward). And the wide-eyed six-year-olds sat quietly and patiently doing their best, even when the teacher wasn't there—all in a language they scarcely understood.

The young teacher was eager and positive. It was difficult getting the students started in English, she said, but "once they catch on, they're off." They had a reading book—one solitary book. The teacher had bought it herself (the DET has no materials in English for the first four grades), and she photocopied every page for every child, binding them into fifty-six books, all with brown-paper covers made by the parents. The book she had chosen was an alphabet colouring book, with "A" and a picture of an apple on the first page, "B" and a boat on the next page (a sailing yacht in Soweto?), and so forth. She got the children to colour in the pictures and copy out the words.

When they started school, none of the children could write. How the teacher got them to hold pencils I don't know, but I could see in their writing books (also homemade, with brown-paper covers and lines drawn by hand by the teacher) their progression from scribbles to something like their names and the numbers. Some could even do the arithmetic problems. The teacher assured me they were learning to understand English. If they were, it must have been mainly "shut up," "keep quiet," and "sit still," because that was what the teacher was urging them to do much of the time. (Is that why older students, even graduate students, speak so quietly?) But they had all learned to chant "Good-morn-ing-teach-er" and "Yes-we-are-very-well-thank-you" because that is the first thing they are all taught to say in every South African school, and they are practised every day.

Later, the two rooms were needed by other classes, so the teacher took her fifty-six students outside for an English lesson. They formed a large circle under a tree and recited "Humpty Dumpty sat on a wall." They also chanted "This is my nose" and "This is my ear."

In a nearby standard 7 (grade 9) Zulu class, the teacher did almost all the talking. The students shared one Zulu text, and all they had to do was provide brief answers to long questions, standing deferentially one at a time to do so.

I talked with the teachers in the staff room. They were friendly and open, like all the South African teachers I met, black and white, and were keen to show off their classrooms. But the work was usually wretched by North American standards. Obviously, these teachers taught the way they had themselves been taught. They tried hard and thought they were doing well, but their resources were pitiful. It was difficult to see these teachers gaining anything from diploma courses in grammar and phonology. They desperately needed an end to their isolation within South Africa and within the world's educational community.

I VISITED ANOTHER RELATIVELY PRIVILEGED DET SCHOOL on the outskirts of Johannesburg, which served students living in or near the troubled township of Alexandra. This school was on the grounds of a prison housing some 4,000 black prisoners of varying degrees of security (prisons are also segregated) and their guards. Originally built as a prison farm school, the premises now accommodated 560 students from grade sub A (grade 1) to standard 6 (grade 8), together with fifteen teachers in fourteen classrooms. Some classes always had to be held under the trees outside. About half the students were the children of prison staff, and half were "outsiders"—mainly the children of domestic servants in surrounding white suburbs.

The energetic principal received little help from the DET, the prison, or nearby white schools. But he had found "sponsors" for a library, in need of replenishment after a theft the previous year. He had also found sponsors for a librarian, who happened to be white (doubly unusual), for a part-time teacher from West Virginia to help the other teachers (unusual again), and for a secretary. But the local sponsors were not keen on a school in a prison, he said, and in any case, they often reduced support after the first year instead of maintaining it. The schools and supportive voluntary organizations tended to prefer funds to donations of books. Books were often dumped on them, said the principal, especially from overseas: "There's only so much we can take about life on Kentucky horse farms."

This school was also in good condition, with large and airy classrooms (overcrowded, of course) and immaculate surroundings (maintained by the prisoners for the prison personnel). But there had been some vandalism to ceilings that the DET would not repair, and the DET would not put safety railings on parts of a raised walkway between some classrooms that was over four feet high.

In accordance with the usual DET practice, English did not become a language of instruction at this school until standard 3 (grade 5). In a standard 1 (grade 3) geography class, I saw fifty-three children busy with their seat work, copying the names of cities from the board into their books and completing blanks in sentences, followed by "corrections." For oral work, they raised their hands if they thought they knew an answer and then stood to speak, even if just one word. The students also stood when anyone entered the room: "Good-morn-ing-tea-cher." "Good morning, standard 3. How are you today?" "We're-very-well-thank-you-tea-cher. How-are-you-today-tea-cher?" "I'm very well thank you. You may sit down."

Another group of over fifty sub B (grade 2) children were doing reading and math in the Sotho language. The teacher wrote a chapter from Genesis on the board in Sotho, and the children copied it into their books. (This was probably reasonable reading practice as the children already knew the words). The teacher also wrote math problems on the board:

$$5 + \Box = 9$$

The children had become expert at filling in the blanks. There were not a lot of repetitions; it took too long to write the problems down. The teacher walked around the crowded class, marking and helping where necessary. The children were typically quiet and industrious, sitting up straight when they had finished their work, which they had already learned to hide uncooperatively from their neighbours while they were writing.

Their textbooks were old, battered, and old-fashioned. The Sotho reading textbook had small illustrations at the top of each page, then half a dozen words broken into syllables and then written in full ("s-e, s-w-a, s-w-i, seswaswi, s-e-s-w-a-s-w-i"), and then a dozen long sentences containing quite long words. It didn't look easy. There were no phonics. The English language reading book was also essentially word attack, with illustrations of white children engaging in white activities, key words, and disconnected sentences.

The standard 4 (grade 6) English textbook claimed to give students "some confidence" in reading and writing English. It had short reading passages, miserable black and white illustrations, and many fill-in-the-blanks exercises, jumbled sentences, and comprehension questions.

There were some decorations on classroom walls: letters of the alphabet, shapes, colours, and fruits. There were also pictures of children and adults, usually white, happily working. Black children were featured in posters about malnutrition, drugs, and AIDS.

The library was in a large room with many bare shelves. Everyone was encouraged to borrow books, said the librarian; the children did so, but the teachers wouldn't. There were a few children's books in Sotho and Zulu—usually translations of British or American stories with the original illustrations. The librarian conducted reading groups for all standards in the school.

The principal spoke of the massive differences between neighbouring white schools and black schools in the area: different training, different equipment, and different expectations. Some white schools—even state schools—in his neighbourhood were "like universities" with their swimming pools and gymnasiums. He would like collaboration with white schools; his students learned English from teachers who did not speak the language well, and students in white schools learned Zulu and Sotho from white teachers who didn't speak those languages well. But contacts were rare. There had been resistance from the Transvaal Education Department (the white education authority) when he defied convention and brought a white teacher into his own school, though there was less concern now. He didn't think attitudes were changing very fast.

Teachers needed to be integrated before students, he said. Teachers in white schools did not know what to do with black students or with black teachers, and black teachers would not be able to cope in white schools. Integration should begin in the segregated training colleges.

AT THE UNIVERSITY, a departmental meeting was held to discuss the content of the proposed new third-year course for specialists in English language teaching. The chairperson of the planning group began with a neatly typed list of nine topic headings, seven of which had already been considered and agreed to: methods of linguistic description, language development and cognition, case studies in language education research, critical linguistics, ethnography of South African schooling, history of theories of first- and second-language learning and teaching, and language policies. There were still two to be discussed—literacy, and language and literature—and one to be added ("to make the very satisfying number ten")—contrastive linguistics.

I inquired whether we could provide a rationale for why these particular things should be taught. The collegial calm was shattered. I was told that the rationale had already been sufficiently considered, that staff knew what students needed, and that in any case a rationale was not required, only a "syllabus." The education minister had to have a syllabus to give formal approval to the course and thus to the new department. It was also suggested that rationales were impractical in overcrowded classrooms. And in any case, teachers needed to be taught all these things so they would be "empowered" to make decisions for themselves.

There were other matters to consider. Topics had to be allocated to "levels": Some things should already have been taught in the second year, and some should be withheld until the fourth year. The decision of when something should be taught had to take into account the needs of instructors as well as of students.

It had previously been decided to divide the course into "core" and "elective" elements. A decision had to be made on how each topic should be classified, since all were considered essential. The judgment of Solomon was that all topics should be core and should also be electives; the distinction would be a matter of "depth."

THE MAJORITY OF BLACK STUDENTS AT WITS go into Commerce, where there is a huge failure rate. I had to look hard into the printout of hundreds of first-year examination results on the Commerce Department notice board to find an A. There were a few B's, but masses of F's. The notices seeped hopelessness and discouragement. Students frequently defaced the tables and obliterated their own names to try to wipe out the stain.

A professor from another department told me confidingly: Blacks will never be able to govern; they have no management skills.

LITTLE MORE WAS HEARD IN THE NEWS about cricket after South Africa's victory against mighty Australia was followed by a pair of losses against New Zealand. There was also sobriety in the run-up to the referendum. Unctuous men and women disclosed on television their deepest beliefs about how all South Africa's problems would be solved if only whites could live harmoniously with—or alternatively apart from—what were euphemistically called the black people. There was much reference to the "new situation" in Russia and Eastern Europe, where "different peoples" were clamouring to be released from the domination of "other nations" and there was only bloodshed when they were forced to live together.

Chapter 8

Week Three

MONDAY

After a lunchtime conversation meeting, Joanna tells me she is once more totally confused about the Honours course. She doesn't know what the "agenda" is. I suggest that we discuss it with the group. But at the beginning of the class, I think it might not be a good topic to reopen, so I talk with Joanna separately. She challenges me with just about every possible objection to leaving control of the class to the students.

She is emotional. Her concern is for the others, not for herself. It is the other students who are baffled. They do not seem capable of making decisions for themselves and need guidance. They have been conditioned not to make decisions about teaching. I say that the whole point is to give them experience in making a contribution to their own education. I am not able to guarantee that what they decide will come about for the rest of the year, but I shall present the case on their behalf. I shall argue that they have a valid contribution to make.

But Joanna is afraid that their experience during the first quarter will affect them for the rest of the course. They will not be able to return to being "ordinary students." They need guidance.

I say that if I actively provide guidance, the students will not get the experience they should have, nor will I be able to argue that they are presenting their own point of view. I ask why Joanna doesn't help them herself. She says she cannot talk with them. She is sorry for them but can't help them. She thinks I should intervene even if it destroys everything I am doing—and she approves of what I am doing. Something is going on in the dynamics of the group, though she doesn't know what it is or what to do about it.

"You can't ask the students to do this," she says. "It is too much for them. They have never been taught to do it."

"You mean they have been taught *not* to do it and education has won?" She isn't pleased with this conclusion but assents to it.

I disagree. "Students can be trusted. They *must* be trusted." But she shakes her head. We get nowhere, yet neither of us is able to break off the conversation. She is arguing something I do not understand. Then she begins to rub her eyes. I propose that we go back to the group. She agrees and for the rest of the session is remarkably cheerful, supportive as I get into dilemmas with other students, and sending me glances as if we had some kind of complicit understanding.

I wonder about the source of Joanna's concerns. She is one of the youngest members of the group, though she has worked in a variety of part-time settings in recent years. She is also—with Guy, Marina, and Alice—close to her own undergraduate studies, and probably has a more secure feeling of herself as a student compared with older class members like Laura, Mavis, Albert, and Elizabeth.

Only Mavis, Laura, and Charles are present at the beginning of the class period, apart from Joanna and me. Mavis cannot let the topic of materials production rest. She does not want my advice or my arguments; she wants my approval or capitulation. Joanna had earlier told me I confused students by asking for their ideas and then "slapping them down," the way I had dismissed Mavis's concerns. But now Joanna nods in vigorous agreement when I tell Mavis that materials can't take the place of teaching and that any materials that teachers need they should find or make for themselves, taking into account the particular needs and interests of their own students. No one outside the classroom could tell teachers what materials would be appropriate for their own students. Mavis agrees but says beginning teachers are too unsure of themselves to make their own judgments and need examples to show them what to do. This is the old circular argument again: Teachers and students have no experience with making decisions; therefore, other people have to make decisions for them. Mavis even adds that the "problem" with students is that when shown examples of what they might do, they follow slavishly and do not get ideas of their own. But she still thinks that both teachers and students should be given examples.

Laura agrees. My ideas are impracticable because teachers are so bad. Materials cannot take the place of poor teaching—they can only make the situation worse—but she still thinks that "some" prescriptive materials are necessary. There is no way enough teachers can be improved quickly enough.

I foresee a repetition of my discussion with Joanna. Although Joanna thinks I cannot trust *students* because they have never been trusted before,

Laura and Mavis think *teachers* cannot be trusted for the same reason.

In any case, Laura knows that "materials work." There was an English language project elsewhere in South Africa based on highly prescriptive procedures, and it was successful. How does she know? She read about it somewhere. She has seen children who have been taught in that way, and they know something about English. Not much, but something. They know what they have been taught. I ask if there is not a hidden cost in teaching that teaches something but not much. She supposes there is, but learning something is better than learning nothing.

Laura—usually so clearheaded and open-minded—astounds several of us when she raises some different topics. She thinks all children should learn phonology to help them speak better. Asked how phonology could help anyone to speak better and how people learn to speak in the absence of knowledge of phonology, she says that phonology is about the sounds of language—isn't it?—and that some students don't know the right sounds. I say that students who don't speak the way Laura prefers have learned to speak in some other way. They have still learned sounds, and these sounds are also described by phonology. So how can phonology help them to speak differently?

She changes her tack. Children should learn to speak differently because it affects the way they spell. If children don't speak correctly, they'll never spell correctly. I ask if she thinks that children learn to spell by writing down the sounds of words. Charles adds incredulously, "In English?" She gives an example.

She knows of children who pronounce the word "elephant" as *aliphant.* And they spell it with an initial "a." Charles asks how they spell the *f* sound in the middle, and she says "ph"—she doesn't know how they learned that. And I ask how they spell the *ant* at the end when the pronunciation is a schwa—a sound that can be represented by a, e, i, o, or u. She says they can learn the correct spelling. So why does it matter whether they say elephant or aliphant if they have to learn how to spell the word in any case? She makes a sideways move again.

"How can you learn to spell any word if you don't pronounce it correctly?" she asks rhetorically. "You wouldn't even know that the name 'Harry' is spelt h-a-r-r-y."

I can scarcely believe what I'm hearing. Laura has stumbled on a classic linguistic example of a phonemic difference that may not be phonetic. "Do you know what I thought you said?" I ask. "I thought you said 'hairy'—spelt h-a-i-r-y."

"I did," says Laura. "'Hairy'—spelt h-a-r-r-y."

"You know that many people would think you had said the word spelt h-a-i-r-y?" I say.

"Of course I know," she replies. "I'm South African. That's the way we say it."

She laughs. She recognizes the illogicality of the argument but nevertheless thinks it makes a valid point. You need to know phonology in order to spell and you need to know grammar in order to speak properly; members of the staff have taught these assertions to students quite vigorously and obviously successfully. Like Mavis, Laura is a particularly intelligent and dedicated teacher with considerable classroom and university experience. She would usually be considered well educated. But she has not had the reflective experience of testing her assumptions—or those of her academic teachers—beyond the daily question of whether they justify her activities. I think that perhaps Joanna was right: that "education" has won and that teachers have learned not to look critically at anything.

TUESDAY

Sixteen students arrive for the Honours meeting: Laura, Mavis, Joanna, Guy, Marina, Alice, Thomas, Charles, Faith, Deirdre, Eleanor, Gertrude, Albert, Bonnie, Brandon, and Benjamin. The only absentee is Elizabeth, whose daughter had her jaw broken when youths pulled her down the stairs of a bus. The students have not established habitual places in which to sit in the room. They select seats on the basis of interest, drawn to each other by common concerns or by chance, where they happen to have been standing. There is no indication of age, gender, or colour segregation. But there is concern that the smaller groups are becoming isolated by the topic categories they have chosen.

Guy and Joanna open with an assault on the way they think the groups have separated themselves into separate topic areas, such as cognition, language acquisition, skills, and language and power. They have ideas on how groups should pool their "experiential knowledge." They also want people to prepare and share "personal profiles" about themselves, their professional environment, and their fundamental beliefs about education and about what promotes learning—an idea adopted from the morning session. They think this information will help them to understand the resources of the group. They even want to put up a "photo board with ID pictures of everyone." Guy is very keen on people getting to know each other so that they can understand and respect their different points of view.

Joanna has shifted the focus of her anxiety from individuals to "groups." She is concerned with the "mobility" of groups and wants to set up "telephones" among them. Also, she says, some people don't know why they are reading. There should be more speculation within groups about what they might get from their reading. They should look at what other groups have read or would like to read. Could the groups be trusted? She did not get a very supportive reaction.

Deirdre objects that they will all be giving papers to one another in a couple of weeks in any case and that they have enough work for now. (This is the first I have heard of papers being prepared.)

Guy: "We don't want any group to have a hidden curriculum. We don't want any coups d'états" (mystifying most of the other students).

Charles, reading from extensive notes, intervenes with a scheme of his own that covers their activities to the end of the year. He thinks they have been "trying to catch fish in a chamberpot" with all the questions the groups are generating. He suggests pooling questions and having brainstorming sessions with the entire staff. When the questions have been "condensed and consolidated" by various "task forces," they could be the basis of a series of symposia conducted by invited staff in the second and third quarters, followed by discussions. In the final quarter, more task groups could prepare comprehensive documents to edit and circulate for the benefit of students in future years.

Charles is asked why he wants to invite the staff in to give their point of view en masse. He says the staff have the advantage of hindsight: They've been giving the course for years and "know what works."

Guy: "That's precisely what we want to avoid. We want the experience of everyone in the group feeding in, not approval from the staff."

Deirdre wants to know what the school visits they have been making have to do with "all this discussion."

Charles: "The visits inform our discussions."

Guy renews his appeal for personal portfolios: "Whenever we have a discussion, we have misunderstanding. If we know who a person is, then we will have some kind of understanding."

Joanna objects very strongly that she is not being heard. No one understands what she has been trying to say. She goes to the chalkboard and takes charge. She draws a large unlabelled circle in the center, connected by sweeping lines to a circle labelled "personal portfolios" on the left and a cluster of circles labelled "groups" on the right. The personal element on the left consists of an "experiential pool," she explains.

Deirdre interrupts. She would like to have discussion and agreement on parts of the diagram before moving on. But Joanna wants to complete her entire picture and forces her way ahead over Deirdre's objections.

Joanna turns her attention to the "groups" on the right of the diagram. She sees two large groups—language acquisition and skills—which need a "group dynamics policy." They need to *document* their process and thus should appoint a chairperson and a note taker.

Between the groups and the individuals, the central circle is now labelled to indicate "feedback—communication between groups—work is pooled." Joanna presents all of this very earnestly, assuming that it makes more immediate sense to the group than it does.

She thinks each of the four groups should determine its own hypotheses. For example, they might ask why they think the study of cognition might be helpful or why they want to study language and power. Would it help them to study linguistics? Groups should document what they read and should write short reviews that could be kept in a cupboard in the room and consulted. It is all part of a complex scheme that Joanna has devised, and for a while she has the full attention of the group. Unless there is some planning, she thinks it will be difficult to produce the papers they are going to write for one another. Joanna says the groups should get more organized and should think about her suggestions.

Stolid Mavis is the first to object. Shouldn't there be talking among everyone in the groups as a whole, not just between the "scribes"?

Alice: "People should deal with what interests them. That's why they're here. Anything that is important will come out of the groups." Joanna demurs; the structure is necessary.

Suddenly, the room is alive. Everyone is involved in the discussion. There are differences of opinion about what they ought to be doing, but they are all focused on the ultimate objective: the design of an Honours course relevant to themselves and future students. There are no cliques, no isolated clusters. For the first time, I realize that everyone has been working, even in the groups that I have seen little of. They have been working constructively and earnestly without any supervision.

Charles leads the opposition to Joanna's notion that the individual groups should intensify their efforts and report through note takers. He wants to know personally what is going on in other groups. Alice says that people can move around if they want to. But she feels strongly that people should stay with their groups; they will stay focused.

Charles and Alice discuss whether vast areas will be uncovered or ignored if initiative is left to individual groups.

Charles reads from his notes again, taking centre stage in place of Joanna, who has been largely ignored in the developing discussion. Charles reasserts his plan for the generation of questions that can be grouped and consolidated by "task forces."

Alice prefers individual presentations by the small groups. She doesn't want consolidation. Papers should be conflicting and should come back to the individual groups for further consideration. There is then a lively logistical discussion about when it will be possible to get the papers completed and circulated.

Charles takes up his point that after questions from all groups have been consolidated, the staff should be brought in for their comments.

Joanna says it hasn't been agreed that the staff should be brought in. The question should be put on the agenda.

Guy wants "personal portfolios" to be provided by staff before staff are brought in. Students should know who the staff are; they need the "cards on the table, face up."

Charles prefers the idea of a party for people to get to know each other.

Marina suddenly asks how they will determine which questions will be worth asking. She thinks the small groups should decide this.

Charles: "The staff will tell us." This is a surprising development in Charles's thinking. Usually, he is emphatic about the value of student opinion. There is a predictable reaction.

Charles persists: "With or without the help of the staff, a task force should put the questions into a logical sequence. There will then be a brainstorming session among staff and students at the end of the present quarter to produce reading lists to be the basis of the following quarter of the course."

Joanna and Laura both want the individual groups to make these decisions.

Alice wants to support Guy's suggestion about personal portfolios from the students, but she doesn't know his name. (Guy says: "Exactly.")

Mavis still doesn't understand why they have to do it.

Guy: "Because there's a lot of power going on here. The same people are doing the talking. Some people don't talk."

Mavis thinks her group has ended its work. They are ready to take their questions to the whole. But Laura disagrees: They still need to meet and talk.

Albert discreetly observes that they are floating around again. The larger group never reaches decisions. Marina also doesn't want a discussion like this every time they all get together.

There is an exchange between Charles and Marina about whether there should be small-group autonomy, and other small discussions start breaking out. Once again, I am impressed by the thoughtfulness of all these discussions. The students have different points of view about procedures, but they take the issues seriously and seek the best. They basically want to develop and share their own learning experiences. I don't see that they need "guidance" from any staff members at this point.

Marina thinks they should just return to work in their groups to prepare their papers, but Charles persists. How will they achieve clarity with lots of little discussions?

Marina wants to know what this "clarity" is—they are just using jargon.

Brandon, conciliatory, proposes that the groups continue. Albert understands that they are leaving it to each group to decide about portfolios. This is tacitly agreed, and they start breaking up into their groups, anxious to get on with their chosen work. I am pleased by the way I was ignored in all of this.

I hand out a request I have prepared asking students if they would send me a statement or letter that sets out their expectations about this part of the course before it started and their thoughts on how the course is going now we are almost halfway through. This would be for archival and documentary purposes among ourselves; if we wait until the quarter ends, we could forget how we felt at the beginning. I am asking my staff colleagues to do the same, and I will write a letter myself. I will circulate letters among the group if individual writers agree. My request is generally accepted, although Joanna is briefly concerned that I might see other people's letters before writing my own or before sharing them—as if that might be some kind of advantage or privilege. I agree not to look at any of the letters before writing my own and not to circulate any of them until all that are coming in have been received. I suggest we might collect all the responses but not look at them until the course is over. Joanna does not think that is necessary. "The important thing is to get the information," she says. "It wouldn't hurt to share it immediately, and it might satisfy some curiosity."

We take away with us copies of Charles's document, which will be the basis of all his arguments throughout the quarter. Like Joanna, he seems to have a deep personal involvement in the proceedings that drives him to organize everyone else. His idea is that every group and every individual—with the cooperation of staff—would generate a "multitude of questions" to be organized and consolidated by "task groups." A joint session of all the students and staff would then attempt to assess which questions are likely to yield the most fruitful discussion, and a task group or plenary session would order the questions into a logical sequence. A brainstorming session of staff and students would generate a list of worthwhile readings into which students might delve before the next step, which would be a weekly symposium on each question, with contributions invited from experts within the group, staff, and others. A general discussion following each symposium would focus on planning strategies for worthwhile research to be delegated to task groups or individuals. Every student would then write a preliminary response to all or a selected number of the symposia, discussions and research. In the final quarter, students would divide into task groups, take all the personal responses, and consolidate them into a more comprehensive document or article for possible publication in a kind of yearbook—to provide a starting point for next year's group and a consolidation of the year's work.

THURSDAY

After the exhilaration of recent meetings, the group today seems very thin and flat. Several members are missing, but perhaps they are busy elsewhere. The others form themselves into the four groups very quickly and quietly. Mavis is now anxious about "comprehension skills" because her daughter has been having some trouble with her teacher. I say that comprehension skills are a fiction and that a lack of understanding simply means that something doesn't make sense to Mavis's daughter, not that there is an intellectual defect.

Mavis says: "I thought you'd say that." She had hoped there might be some better questions the teacher could ask instead of the particular "comprehension questions" she was using.

I suggest that the problem might be the practice of asking questions every time the student reads something. Mavis can't think what else the teacher might do. How could the teacher know her daughter had learned anything?

Laura wants to know how psychology became so involved in education. She is reading a book about psychology and teaching reading and doesn't understand what the relationship is. Why should educators listen to psychologists?

But she is also interested in personality and "affective factors." Aren't these involved in learning in some way? I say of course: People's personalities make a difference to how they learn particular things, and so do their feelings—whether they are confident or insecure, interested or bored, energetic or lethargic, collaborative or resentful. She knows this, but now she thinks she should read what psychologists have to say on the topic. I ask what she thinks psychologists might know that novelists or teachers themselves would not know and would probably discuss in more comprehensible terms.

The second-year group—Marina, Alice, and Thomas—are working away, as they often do, in a separate room. Alice tells me later that they don't feel much in common with the other group; they feel they "missed out" last year and don't see much scope to change things for themselves for the rest of this year. They are studying cognition because of mutual interest. They are all concerned with learning, especially with the difficulties of black students.

Back with the other groups, I outline my comments on Vygotsky, expanding on his concept of a constantly shifting *zone of proximal development* within which learning takes place (with help) but outside which no learning is possible. The idea attracts some interest, and zone of proximal development is soon reduced to the initials ZPD. Questions arise like: "Aren't there stages in learning second language that move things outside the ZPD?" and "Does this apply to people of all ages?" Laura wants to know whether some things might *stay* in the ZPD. People might be able to do such things with help but would never be able to do them independently—for instance, herself and bookkeeping.

Deirdre, sitting by herself, asks about "the relation" between learning and age. A piano teacher had told her that many people stop learning at about seventeen.

Chapter 9

Possibilities

I visited an "inner-city" white school with an exemplary reputation, the kind of place visitors to South Africa are readily shown. It was a model B school that "opened" to nonwhite students the previous year, located in an eastern suburb of Johannesburg with a superb view across to a gold mine and its dumps. The 600-pupil school, from grade sub A to standard 5 (grades 1 to 7) served a large Portuguese local population. There were also some Greek students and a few Korean students, but so far the only black students were a couple from Zaire, not local. English was the sole language of instruction at the school, and every effort was made to ensure that students who initially did not understand the language were helped at least to understand what was going on.

The head teacher was considered by the staff to be "progressive" and tried to recruit well-qualified young teachers. The school was relatively well off for computers and science equipment (from "donations"), but most of their books were wretched. Parents paid about eighty Rand (about forty U.S. dollars) a term for fees and, I was told, typically refused to pay more (if they did not default altogether), so students did not get many new books.

The school routine was South African traditional: Uniformed students stood to chant a greeting whenever anyone entered the classroom, no matter what they and the teacher were doing, and they stood to address the teacher. Quite a few students were standing outside the classrooms or in the stairwells with their noses against the wall for "punishment." The general impression was of a happy school but a strict one, with "well-behaved" students.

The staff had read or heard a little of contemporary educational practices in Europe and North America (like "whole language," which they thought they were exemplifying), but the consequences of the long-enforced isolation of South African teachers were apparent. Their classwork in reading, writing, and mathematics struck the visitor as narrow and unimaginative—particularly the American mathematics and reading software programmes they were using on their computers. Every activity was dominated by exercises and marks. Yet, the staff regarded themselves as advanced; no doubt they were in comparison with many other South African schools.

THERE ARE MANY SMALL, INFORMAL INITIATIVES centred on or around the university to improve education. An "ESL forum" was held in the Education Department, attended by forty mainly white primary school teachers. The topic was Teaching English in Multicultural Classrooms.

Some of the participating teachers had been coming to the forum for years, finding support in the exchange of experiences and discussions of ideas. But their concerns, though obviously sincere, seemed to an outsider to be superficial matters that could have been cleared up in the preparation of teachers or in early inservice training. Teachers were worried that black primary pupils could not do "elementary phonics" for their English reading lessons, though they did not know why the pupils might not understand such instruction when it was offered. The pupils could "do words but not sentences," a complaint obviously referring more to classroom busywork than to communication abilities. The pupils also "couldn't do plurals" (that is, put an "s" on the end of a noun in English), which was regarded as a common and critical failing among speakers whose mother tongue was not English.

There was a lot of feeling that black children needed formal English grammar to help them speak better. They also needed more structure than white children in the classroom, because "they don't have any in their lives at home." Sometimes, one teacher complained, they also needed to be introduced to the use of toilets.

SOUTH AFRICAN RESEARCHER SARAH MURRAY (1991) contrasts what she calls "Western" views of learning English (including her own) that require "learner-centred" interactive classroom environments with current practices in black schools and colleges that stress training in "general English language skills."

Of the latter, Murray writes:

> What I have personally observed . . . is, to my way of thinking, an overly
> formal, linguistic approach to the teaching and learning of languages . . .
> but this ignores two fundamental issues relating to language competence.
> Firstly, in the language of the school, English has the functional value of a
> *first language* . . . all their learning must be carried out through the
> medium of English. Secondly, a language is best learned in a meaningful
> context, one in which there is some communicative goal beyond manipula-
> tion of the language itself. Unfortunately this narrow approach to language

learning and teaching does not only apply to English but also to the mother tongue. There are historical reasons for this. . . . The effects of this overly linguistic approach to the teaching of the mother tongue and English have, in my view, been extraordinarily damaging. Both languages have been taught as if they were foreign languages. . . . Firstly, students have been denied access, in the classroom, to the full range of emotional and expressive functions of their mother tongue. In my view, this must have a negative effect on students' motivation, and it must also affect their development in the language itself. Secondly, it has ignored the role played by language in learning, and inhibited the development of the language students need in order to learn their other subjects. Finally, I believe a narrowly linguistic interpretation of language competence has been damaging because it has encouraged the view of the teacher as "the one who knows," "the authority". . . . I have also observed that this formal, linguistic approach to language teaching is frequently accompanied by rote learning methods, which are in part a response to the difficulties of teaching through the medium of a second language. They are also, in my view, a product of a teacher-centred, authoritarian approach to teaching. . . . I have to recognize that [these teaching practices] are deep-rooted and persistent, and presumably informed by beliefs about learning which are different from mine. (p. 7)

Murray quotes Webb (1986), who described student problems she encountered while working at the Soweto College of Education, where black student teachers received diploma training:

The heart of the problem lies not with the difficulty of the text or concepts but with the relationship that exists between a student and his own learning, and with the language of learning. . . . Learning is seldom seen as a subjective experience of moving towards knowledge or coping with the . . . everyday world. It is seen, rather, as achieving through acquiring the proper terms, or language, a body of knowledge that exists outside the mind of the learner as a set of language forms. (p. 8)

Murray comments:

My own feeling is that this view of knowledge arises out of the students' experience of learning, which has been something imposed from outside rather than something generated from within. Surely this cannot be the way to prepare students for participation in a democratic South Africa. (p. 8)

AT WITS, I TOOK THE CENTRAL PART in what I had been told would be a departmental question and answer session on whole language. Instead, I was confronted by several pointed questions about my perceptions of South Africa in the three months since my arrival.

I talked of my unease at the grudging "progress" toward improving the circumstances of the black population, together with great defensiveness about the situation despite expressions of good intention. The university and staff wanted to do better what they were doing already but would not contemplate alternatives. I thought the continual emphasis on "improved teaching and learning" was delusory and would not solve the university's problems. (I was promptly told there were instructors in other departments whose teaching needed plenty of improvement.)

I mentioned the many times I had been told to watch what I was saying, and I was again told I did not understand the situation in South Africa. A colleague said there were issues so sensitive they should not be talked about. When this colleague was in England, there were topics there that people preferred not to talk about.

A black participant spoke emotionally about the "miracle" of learning English in high school despite a complete absence of English and literacy at home and very little English at school until the age of seventeen. But the person did not know by what miracle the learning of English was accomplished. I said this was a question that cried out for research: what exactly goes right when people succeed in learning a language. Typically, one instructional method is compared with another on limited measures of achievement, which throws little light on what might be crucial social and affective factors in coming to embrace an entire language. Fluent black speakers of English in South Africa often talked of extensive reading, but credit was also regularly given to conscientious teachers and intensive study and exercises.

The same person said that reading was a serious problem among black South Africans because they did not come from a "literate culture." They were not in the habit of using libraries freely, and many would never look at a book again after leaving the university—even English students. There was a need to inculcate a culture of literacy.

There was some interest in how whole language might be "applied" in South Africa. I thought it would not be compatible with the prevailing emphasis on ESL instruction as opposed to "bilingual education," in which students would learn to read and write in languages with which they were familiar. There was also a brief discussion of the North American movement to end the discriminatory treatment of individuals by integrating all students into the mainstream, whatever "handicaps" they might have. One colleague emphatically responded that it would be a catastrophe in South Africa: "Teachers wouldn't be able to get through their work."

THERE WERE HIGH HOPES that the department might be able to obtain additional funds to establish a Centre for Applied English Language Studies. Staff and Honours students discussed the form such a centre might take.

The staff at a separate meeting were unanimous in endorsing the idea of a teaching centre located at the university, where more teachers could be taught the right way to teach the English language. Thousands of teachers needed retraining. The staff felt they could not go into actual school districts to work because "uninvited experts" would not be welcomed. But they also thought that the centre would have to award diplomas or certificates (despite all the concerns that would arise about standards and examinations) because black teachers could not be expected to learn without some expectation of reward, either in the form of salary increases or "credit." The favoured model for a centre usually tended to be that of the ESL teaching institutes with which staff happened to have been associated overseas.

A black staff member became suddenly angry: Why did the others always use a Eurocentric model? It was a ubiquitous mistake, trying to fill in a hole without asking local people—always looking overseas instead of looking in South Africa. There was some vehement disagreement with these comments, and the objector withdrew from the discussion.

Students at a combined meeting, on the other hand, thought the centre should be more responsive to teacher interests and concerns. Teachers should be regarded as a resource, not as a problem. Even Soweto teachers had not been overwhelmed by adverse conditions or their horrific history. What they wanted was broader experience, opportunity to exchange knowledge and ideas, and mutual and external support. All of this could be provided by the centre if it was not seen primarily as another place for university instructors to teach.

Students thought the centre should be directed by teacher representatives, not university administrators. It should be located in one or more sites in Soweto and elsewhere in the field, not at the university. One student suggested the centre should be a bus, which could travel around bringing teachers into contact with one another.

But the staff were insistent. The most outspoken saw the centre "ten years down the road" as a replica of International House, a language training institution in London. People came there to become English teachers, said the staff member, and received very basic hands-on training to get a 100-hour diploma in a month. High-powered businessmen also came to the school to bone up on their English. It was "a superb centre, a lively, interesting, and practical place, with no airy fairy nonsense—a language teaching centre."

IN MARCH 1992, A NATIONAL CONFERENCE to discuss the future of education was held at Broederstroom by the ANC, the Congress of South African Trade Unions, the National Educational Crisis Committee, the South African Democratic Teachers' Union, and other black or nonracial organizations.

They were concerned with the need to restore a "culture of learning."

Their sanguine decisions included willingness to engage with existing government structures; this was a new attitude after the events of the mid-1980s, which mainly drew students out of schools through boycotts and demonstrations. But they would resist the unilateral restructuring of schools by the government (such as putting all existing white schools under local community control). They wanted a single education department for the country, equitable per capita expenditure on all students, serious efforts to end violence in schools, and new curricula based on nonracism and nonsexism "to prepare students for a democratic society." They also wanted special emphasis on *redress*—particularly for blacks, the disabled, women, the unemployed, and those in rural communities. Education should work to build a national democratic culture, with diversity preserved "so long as it does not conflict with other key principles." There was a concern with "empowerment" but no resolution about language.

A TUTORIAL GROUP MET INSTRUCTORS to provide feedback on the second-year course so far. The "information sheet" devised for that purpose by the staff was criticized as soon as it was handed out: Why did they need to know the sex of respondents and their date of birth?

The document also wanted to know "mother tongue." Out of nineteen students, the following were reported: Afrikaans, English, Greek, Northern Sotho, Setswana, Shangaan, Southern Sotho, Tsonga, Tswana, and Zulu. The following were reported as "other languages spoken": Ndebele, Pedi, Sepedi, Shona, Swazi, and Venda, as well as Italian and (reading only) classical Greek and Latin.

One black student claimed to speak nine languages, and several others claimed four or five. Three languages were not uncommon. No black students spoke just one African language and nothing else or English and nothing else, and no white students could speak any indigenous language.

The nineteen students split almost stereotypically in evaluating the course. Several black students, male and female, wanted more grammar: They would have to teach grammar and wanted to be shown how to do it. The question came down to: "How will we know how to teach the pronoun?" White students, who were not expecting to teach English, preferred the aspects of the course that dealt with such topics as language and society and language and power. One said: "We don't need all this talk about 'bound morphemes'; we know how to talk." White students were also not happy at "being treated like ESL students."

Black students in general did not see the point of doing assignments that were not marked. "We came to university to get grades; isn't that what it's all about?"

A DAY OF GREAT EXCITEMENT IN JOHANNESBURG, with radios and televisions turned on continuously in every office, and crowds around television store windows in the streets. The occasion was an international cricket match between South Africa and England, which South Africa lost on the penultimate ball of the game.

There were no crowds for the other main item in the news: a rash of violence around Johannesburg, especially in the township of Alexandra. There, the score was more than eighty people killed over a few days in tribal (or political) violence, a church set on fire, people killed on or thrown off moving trains, and a couple "necklaced."

The violence was a bleak prelude to the following week's referendum, with all sides talking of the chaos that would result if the vote went against them. There was talk of civil war if there was a "no" majority.

Chapter 10

Week Four

THURSDAY

I return from a brief visit to Cape Town, a serene city in a brilliant setting embraced by two oceans that Johannesburg never sees. But at the Art Gallery, I saw violence and chaos were in all the contemporary paintings and sculpture—such unrelieved anger and bitterness.

LAURA, REMEMBERING MY APPREHENSIONS, offers me immediate reassurance that the students have been "working" in my absence. They would come up with proposals for the course, even though I have been told by a couple of well-meaning colleagues that the class is "floundering" and that I should revert to lecturing. The experience is well worthwhile, says Laura, even though they are quite unused to it—and the occasional floundering will not hurt anyone.

We discuss the propensity of students and of staff to attribute knowledge to authority—to books and "experts"—rather than to their own judgment and experience. They try to accommodate authoritative pronouncements into what they do, usually tenuously and impractically, rather than to employ their own common sense and experience to assess the relevance of what they are told. Laura says: "We can't help it. It's always been that way." I tell her once again that South Africa is not unique.

Faith has been to Eleanor's school and was surprised by the relaxed atmosphere and variety of activities there. Faith attended a "Chinese school" in Johannesburg, but all the instruction was in English except for "Mandarin as a subject." She learned her fluent English there, she thinks, but the teaching was very rigid. She wonders now what she did actually learn there and how the teaching had been accomplished.

The skills group has invited a staff member to talk about materials development. The instructor does this in an easy conversational way, encouraging the group to describe the materials they use in their own classrooms. But this is scene setting, the establishment of rapport. The discussion does not go beyond descriptions of what the students do to any consideration of what the students *think.* Their comments are immediately related to the instructor's well-formulated personal point of view, and the students *listen.* The students take notes; the instructor does not.

The instructor wants to distinguish "materials development" from what publishers and curriculum developers do, retaining the term only for the classroom context. According to this argument, materials development involves transforming "materials" (e.g., books) into "activities" (e.g., children talking about books). There is a language problem here when people try to save a controversial term like "materials development" (or "evaluation" or "failure") by giving it their own idiosyncratic meaning, not recognizing that they thereby validate commercial or manipulative activities that carry the same label. The world will not change through attempts to define how language should be interpreted.

The same instructor is critical of prescribed textbooks—a politically correct position these days—and points out that many people think such books are disempowering for teachers. South African teachers are often sent one textbook to which they are chained for a year—Gertrude interpolates "forever"—in their teaching. The books and the way they are used are very top-down and authoritarian.

Elizabeth is enthusiastic about independent reading; it is through reading that children's learning is enhanced. She wants more books and other materials in her Soweto classroom. (Mavis looks at me challengingly, as she does every time "materials" are mentioned.) But Elizabeth wants her students to exercise initiative. She got them to produce a code of conduct for their own behaviour in school: whether they should smoke, drink, or carry weapons in the classroom.

The instructor asks the group how they feel when a box of textbooks is delivered to their classroom from their education departments. Elizabeth says she will only use the books if she wants to, and Albert and Brandon agree. But Gertrude says she would have to follow the books. If the inspectors insisted that she teach page 24 by the end of the week, that is what she would have to do.

Mavis, with another sideways glance at me, asks if textbooks have ever given any other students good ideas or informed them about modern theory.

Brandon: "No. They're universally useless."

Albert: "Once you take a book, you're stuck with it. The DET won't take it back. They've been refusing to change one teacher's book since 1985."

But Gertrude and Brandon think that teachers have more freedom now.

Albert, always quietly critical of teachers, says they often tend to lose direction without a textbook. They lose confidence.

The visiting instructor suggests students ask themselves what vision of teaching is contained in a prescribed textbook.

Mavis (finding the correct answer): "It makes us subject to the system and to the people making money out of it."

Instructor (emphatically): "Right."

Albert: "It makes teachers think that everything to be learned is covered in the book."

Instructor: "All the power is in the textbook. It takes the creativity away from teachers."

Brandon says that he tells his students that the textbook is just one item in their learning and that he gets them to bring in black newspapers. He is also building a library of cartoons to engage his students in language and thinking. They can relate political cartoons to their own experience. But the examinations are based on the textbook, and if he doesn't use the book, his students do badly. The students know more with the newspaper, but they do less well.

Mavis, recapitulating an earlier point: "Aren't there *new* materials which give theory and new ideas to teachers?"

Albert, again: "Teachers get dependent on the materials they have got. It's hard to get them to change. Older teachers rely on older materials. They resist new materials because they don't want to change their attitudes."

Brandon thinks that since the mid-1980s, textbooks have become more relevant. There has been a whole shift of thinking for whites as well as for blacks. "Who is behind this?" he asks.

The instructor admits to producing an English series for a publisher, aiming to have an African bias and to change racial thinking.

Mavis returns to a basic point: "How do you get a confident, resourceful teacher?"

Brandon says he is tired of all this talk of teachers being constrained by the system: "Let's break out of it." (Is he referring to the talk or to the system?)

Mavis, doggedly, wants to discuss the development of materials as part of the course. I leave the conversation at this point, but it goes on, as I suspect it has gone on for several weeks.

DURING THE DISCUSSION, Brandon has been walking quietly around the room informing everyone that he will be on television this evening and giving the station and the time. He is a leader of a protest against something concerning his school. In a brief clip seen this evening, he speaks fluently and confidently in English, although the report containing the interview is only broadcast on a vernacular channel.

RESPONSES TO MY REQUEST FOR REACTIONS to the Honours course are beginning to come in. The following are some extracts, written three or four weeks after the beginning and not read by anyone until the end:

> It was an approach that was very different from what I've experienced at Wits or anywhere else. I was excited about it—but this feeling was often coupled with one of anxiety. . . . Thank you for asking us to do this.

> The course is exciting and very interesting. I am quite motivated. I realize that my contributions towards designing the course are very essential. I am pleased and impressed that expression of thought is encouraged. I also appreciate the fact that there is respect for everyone's opinion. . . . The attitude of some other classmates towards some of us is disturbing, like pinpointing the passiveness of others . . . there should be respect for one another.

> The interviews and entrance tests were perfectly horrifying . . . the department's representatives at the interview actually went as far as *warning* me that "there will be a lot of reading" in this course, and that I should consider dropping all my extramural activities whilst doing Honours. It was an odd demand, I thought, as all of these "extramural activities" involved TEACHING. How on earth can one study something that you don't do? . . . I regarded the experiment with utmost suspicion and you in particular as the Dr. Frankenstein of an inevitable disaster. I saw the people in the group as irreparably "disempowered" and the hierarchies in the university as monuments to contemporary culture. . . . BUT: I slowly but surely shifted again. I started to sense that everybody in the group was going through similar motions and that a bit of intrasupport therapy was in order. . . . Finally, my sense of the project as a whole is that it is the best thing that has hit this university—ever. Education in this country has been such a mess for so many years . . . that sticking to any old formula is but a short-term "resolution."

> The unusual, exploratory nature of the first part of the course seems to me to have resulted in progress in fits and starts. . . . Sometimes it is difficult to get consensus or to gain concretely from what

we have discussed during plenary sessions, but we do seem not to be finding direction during group work and reaching a state where we can constructively share our ideas. Initially . . . it was easy to feel that we were floundering.

Original Expectations: I had expected to be involved with other students in sharing our experiences as language teachers and trying to build on what we had in common. . . . I never thought that we would be into the third week and still be seeking a way forward. *Current Perception:* Sometimes I think I enjoy the excitement of planning a course . . . but at other times I wish I could be studying and increasing my knowledge of teaching English to students. . . . I would also prefer to have the lecturer come forward and give some direction.

In the selection test we did in November . . . we read a long and intimidating (for me) chapter on syntax and had to answer some difficult (for me) questions in the test. I actually got quite panicky. . . . I approached February with some trepidation. I was therefore both surprised and excited when you made your proposal that we design our own course. It was a very liberating feeling and I came away from that first meeting feeling quite elated. . . . The significant turning point came when you walked out of the class. . . . I was amazed at how quickly we got going after that; it was a kind of catalyst, a release from the inertia that comes from waiting for teachers/lecturers/professors to tell you what to do. . . . Of course, it's been a difficult and sometimes painful process. Freedom is a heady thing; I've been on a kind of "high" most of the three weeks—mentally hyperactive, my head spinning, looking for focus and direction, picking up one book and then another, unable to sleep. . . . I found the last session on Tuesday uncomfortable because of the rising of tensions and tempers. I did not like the competitive, almost aggressive atmosphere that emerged. . . . Why do some people talk too much and others too little?

My original thoughts on the Honours course included *inter alia* highly pedagogic and serious grammar learning. I imagined philosophical and pristine linguistic excellence coupled with cognitive and methodological development. I felt personal trepidation about the course, as if I had to cross some "academic rubicon". . . . Well, the course so far has turned out to be exciting and kind of humbling . . . for the first time in my academic life, I have found myself reading furiously without any assignment looming in the

horizon. . . . In my community, education has been hugely dis-
astrous and unproductive, authoritarian, and officious. Pupils have
had a view of a monster that has to be tackled. . . . Irrelevant syllabuses and ill-equipped and unmotivated teachers are factors that
still haunt most classrooms. . . . With the severe socioeconomic
deprivations, most pupils took up political issues with great fervour.
Education became a mere slogan. . . . It seems to me that the
Honours course is pioneering the way . . . the course proceedings, as we have them now, are indeed futuristic.

I must admit that your approach threw me into a confused state of
mind, that I even thought of withdrawing from the course immediately, and the simple reason was that it was a radical turn from the
known system, and myself as a drenched South African student—
used to the top-bottom kind of authority in almost all spheres of
existence—found it to be quite incomprehensible. . . . It is defi-
nitely a novel approach because the student—particularly the
experienced teacher—is given a real opportunity of thinking about
the problems that he/she may be or could have encountered at
work. I think it is quite advantageous to the whole group to share
each other's experiences. . . . However, it must be realized that
to the majority of the students on the course, the approach is still
strange and not readily embraceable in a comfortable manner
because of the educational background and a myriad of more hin-
dering factors.

Having been given [the previous year's reading list in advance of the
course] . . . I started reading. Some of it was fascinating, but some
of it, like advanced phonetics and phonology, made me sympathize
with the comment that experts learn more and more about less and
less until they know everything about nothing. The thought of having to examine and remember such trivia . . . brought me to our
first meeting rather chastened, somewhat apprehensive, and certainly less enthusiastic. At our first meeting, my hopes were revived.
. . . When, as today, we seem to be arguing at cross-purposes, I
become disheartened . . . but I still believe we'll muddle through
to something worthwhile—not to the very best we might have
achieved, but nonetheless much better than we might have done
under the old system. . . . I have no doubt that you are encountering a great deal of resistance to your approach, much of it bitter,
petty, vindictive, and thoroughly ignorant. . . . Whatever happens, this is going to be a very interesting year. Even if the course

turns out to be an unmitigated disaster, we shall have learned valuable lessons, ones that perhaps can be learned in no other way.

My thoughts on how the course is proceeding vary from week to week. At times I feel that we are making progress towards our decided goal, and at others I feel we are floundering somewhat aimlessly. There is a sense of uncertainty within the group as to what we are aiming at and whether we will succeed in achieving anything worthwhile. . . . As a teacher, I appreciate being considered to have thoughts on language teaching and experiences that are of value. . . . Although I feel intellectually challenged to the point of being vulnerable at times, I am not feeling unsure about where I am going or what I am aiming to do during this seven-week period. We come from very diverse backgrounds and have a lot to share with one another.

From a student letter at the end of the course:

The way in which the class both explicated its experience and posed solutions was unsystematic and often arbitrary. . . . [We] worked almost entirely in a vacuum, confined largely by the limits of our own experience and without guidance. . . . There was a gender split with the women speaking very little. Clearly, this was also linked to the question of race. . . . It is not sufficient, I believe, . . . to assume that the students themselves would put it right . . . these are extremely sensitive issues in S.A., and that is why sometimes only the person in the role of the gatekeeper/guider can make such interventions. . . . I have serious questions as to whether it was the appropriate approach, given the particular conjuncture that the Honours programme, the university, and the country find themselves in.

Mid-course staff comments included:

A major challenge of the Honours course has always been that there is so much work on a wide front and that students come with relatively little relevant background. It was the first course of its kind in the country, and the course design (and methods) have been fairly conservative because of our own experience and that of most of our students. . . . There has generally been a consensus about the content of the course, though we have often discussed the weight which should be given to individual components. It has been a taught course, generally informed by the courses which the tutors had taken in their own applied linguistics degrees. . . . I recall [my instructor] starting my introductory course by saying that it had a simple aim: to help people to read the literature in the field, and that remains a useful guideline.

My original understanding of the way in which this process would work was that the staff would be more involved in this experiment than they turned out to be. I think this is a pity. . . . there are inherent problems in this syllabus type which exist regardless of the learners' education backgrounds. One of the problems is with democracy and choice. Once the majority decide to embark on this process, what position do the minority, who may decide at some point that what they have agreed to is not what they want, have in the class? . . . Apartheid has instilled a culture of silence and domination which we are fighting to overcome. The classroom is one arena in which this battle can be won. And the teacher/facilitator's role is to create the conditions for this by ensuring that *everyone's voice* is heard.

Other staff made comments about the course that they were not willing to have shared or published in any way.

Chapter 11

Signs of Hope

C ompared with the ravaged site where Albert taught, Elizabeth's school on the other side of Soweto, though stark and reformatory-like, was an oasis. There were fewer students, more teachers, more classrooms, and fewer signs of vandalism. There was a functioning (though woefully under-equipped) library, solid doors, barred windows (most with their panes), and fewer holes in the ceilings (although the library lost all its books a year before through its ceiling). There were efforts to decorate some classroom walls with maps and pictures. The staff room had an electric kettle, and there was a copier. There was even a school secretary.

But it was still not a school where learning or teaching might be thought easy. The world pressed hard against it. Small children, dogs, and other intruders were able to push through holes in the boundary fence from the mean houses and shacks outside. Dust was everywhere—grass is scarce in Soweto because there is little water—and it was hard to distinguish the arid school yard from the unpaved roads outside. Dead bodies had lain along these roads in recent months, and students had to pass them on the way to school. And symbols of violence were present in the school, including graffiti that the staff would not remove on exterior classroom walls: "COSAS," "MK," and "AK-47" (referring to the black South African student organization, the armed wing of the ANC, and the rifle).

Many teachers still had not recovered from the 1970s and 1980s, when they were caught in the middle between militant students and repressive administrations. Underpaid, undertrained, and unprepared for horrendous discipline problems, they had to be agents of a hated regime, with a constant fear of classroom informers waiting for them to make statements contrary to official policies. Yet, there was a spirit of hope among staff and students that at some time, somehow, things might get better. One wondered where the optimism and the incredible generosity of spirit came from.

Students were returning to school. That was a good sign. Elizabeth was getting her students to practise speaking English, despite a racket from the adjacent class through open doors and windows. The topic she had chosen, typical for Elizabeth, was friendship. Elizabeth was a whole-language teacher without ever having heard of whole language. She had put her students into "writers' groups" of four at desks moved to face one another, an unusual arrangement in South African schools. She encouraged her students to write of their experiences, seeing it as a form of catharsis. Elizabeth's great personal concern was child abuse, another enormous problem in the townships. But like AIDS, it was a topic that many teachers, parents, and the DET believed should not be discussed in schools. There was a strong general feeling of what constituted appropriate subject matter for classrooms, and Elizabeth could not escape it. The writing books of her students were replete with definitions of irony, hyperbole, and other technical aspects of the English language, with examples carefully copied from workbooks and exercises exhaustively completed.

A girl volunteered to tell a story and recited by heart a lengthy account of the birth of Jesus. The other forty teenagers in the class listened in respectful silence as she told her long story, and they applauded at the end. Like the Afrikaans language itself, Western religions flourished most in South Africa in nonwhite communities.

In another classroom, a teacher who was also a poet took a class through one of his own poems. He spoke clear and fluent English in an oddly accented manner with mispronunciations of "rhymes" like "lover," "hover," "mover," and "rover." His extensive experience of English had obviously been largely limited to reading—reinforced, possibly, by courses on English phonology.

ON THE DAY BEFORE THE REFERENDUM, there were many predictions from media commentators and from both the "yes" and "no" sides that violence would follow the result, whatever it might be. State President de Klerk was saying this would be the last time that whites alone would vote on any issue. Would this help toward a "yes" vote? And the violence grew, in any case: Over a hundred people were killed during the previous week in "intraracial bloodshed," which de Klerk said (inaccurately) would decrease if there was a "yes" vote. And always bobbing up above the political discussions was the sports news, keeping the names of commercial sponsors as prominent as those of referendum politicians. South Africa had got to the semifinals of a world cricket contest, and a South African came fifth in an international power boat race.

ON A RADIO CALL-IN PROGRAMME, an ANC spokesperson explained that ANC proposals (not yet policy) rejected the concept of "official languages." They

wanted "just recognition" and full development for all eleven "major lan-
guages" of the country (out of an estimated total of twenty-two languages):
Afrikaans, English, Sesotho, Seswati, Sindebele, Sipedi, Tsonga, Tswana,
Venda, Xhosa, and Zulu.

But most callers wanted to argue that English was so internationally and
economically important that it had to be the "linking language," the lingua
franca, the one essential and primary tongue. The ANC speaker rejected this
"linguistic dominance" view and wanted to know "which English" had to be
learned. Why not Black English?

Several English and Afrikaner callers also wanted whites to learn a black
language as a kind of act of expiation or a quid pro quo, though it would be
of little practical use to most of them and was contrary to all the arguments
put forward about the dominance of English. Perhaps it was expected to help
whites understand what it might be like for blacks to have to learn three or
more languages, which many of them do, or to learn a badly taught language
that meant nothing to them.

Someone inquired how a united South Africa could be built on a frag-
mentation of languages. But the speaker did not believe language could be
used to unite people. There seemed to be a general desire to maintain individual "language rights," but no one specified what these were and how they
could be maintained. No one claimed to have practical "solutions"—only
strong opinions. Among whites, there were frequent objections to "idealis-
tic" planning, and among blacks, objections to "Eurocentric" attitudes.

ACROSS TOWN FROM SOWETO, Codesa delegates were told that English should
be the main language in South Africa and that the only practicable form of
English for official use was "standard British English." The other ten important South African languages could have varying kinds of secondary status.
The speaker was the president of the English Academy of Southern Africa.

PAULSTON (1987) ARGUES THAT LANGUAGE is almost never the cause of
exploitation or illiteracy, but a result or mirror of social conditions generally.
Success in learning or literacy does not depend on which language is used as
the medium of instruction in schools but on overriding outside social and
economic factors. Smith (1989) also proposes that the value of literacy is
overrated and the social consequences of its absence exaggerated.

THE RESULT OF THE REFERENDUM surprised many people, with over 85 per
cent of the eligible electorate voting almost 70 per cent to 30 per cent in
favour of continuing the Codesa talks. Many students and staff were
euphoric, with some white students whooping as they came into classes,
shaking hands with black students and behaving as if a great victory had been

won. Blacks were more restrained but relieved. Much of South Africa breathed again.

It was a day of symbols. As the president offered a half apology for apartheid, the Johannesburg skies were rent by crashing thunder and lightning. The long national drought was broken by torrential rains. Black Zimbabwe, which had not previously won an international cricket match, beat lofty England. The world had turned upside down. Why such a vote and such a turnaround? Theories included a fear of civil war, the threat of further sanctions and total economic collapse, fatigue, a desire to swallow bitter medicine, and even—a few sanguine blacks and whites dared to hope—some seeds of mutual trust and goodwill.

EXTENSIVE TERRORISM CONTINUED on commuter trains in the townships and around worker hostels in Soweto and Alexandra. As usual, the violence was blamed on ANC and Inkatha Freedom Party extremists, with police or security force complicity or provocation suspected. Alexandra residents were threatening a "stay home" from work if no official action was taken to prevent violence. This would affect several university staff. Some cleaners were staying home because a black taxi in which they were coming to work was shot at and a woman passenger alongside them killed.

There was postreferendum talk in the media about the possibility of a right-wing coup with the support of the army or the police. But fewer than half of the lower ranks of the police are white, and there had been efforts to move the army more effectively under civilian control in recent months.

Prominent in the news were reports from neighbouring Zimbabwe that the government would expropriate millions of hectares of white farmland and the farms themselves, with little or no compensation, in order to settle a million black peasants. It was the kind of action that roused deep fears in white South Africa about the consequences of a black government.

A WHITE STUDENT DROVE ME HOME and asked if I found South Africans a suspicious people. They had grown up in an atmosphere of mistrust and were not used to being given responsibility for their own actions. Even liberal whites knew they had been living comfortably off the fruits of apartheid. And they were all angry with the rest of the world for its condemnation and the crippling economic sanctions.

Interracial collaboration in South Africa was not new, the student continued. There was a long history of individual blacks and whites fighting together against apartheid and for a black franchise and an even longer history of them fighting together against the general social and economic discrimination against blacks and other groups. There had been strong movements toward integration and racial collaboration in the trade unions, and blacks and whites worked together in many professional roles in universities and in hospitals. But too few blacks were involved, and although some were in positions of authority and responsibility, the majority were at the bottom, where they had always been. The Wits law department was making a special effort to try to produce a thousand black lawyers. There was a great need for a total overhaul of education, health, and other social services and for the establishment of multicultural neighbourhoods. There were problems for everyone, not just politicians. But people were used to a coercive, paternalistic regime.

THE FOLLOWING EXTRACTS are from the writing of students aged sixteen and seventeen in Soweto high schools. I thank the authors, who will know who they are. The extracts are reproduced exactly as they were written, with the original spelling, capitalization, and punctuation retained and the teacher's red-ink corrections omitted. The first extract was an unmarked piece of independent writing by a young man with literary ambitions, written in Zulu and translated for his teacher by the author. The "uniforms" to which he refers are the distinctive shirt, tie, and skirt or trousers outfits, relics of colonial days that are still worn by students in all South African schools. The other three extracts were class assignments.

The Day of confusion in our school

We were gathered in our school yard as usual for praying. We were puzzled by a lass which was crying in a sad manner. Then the deligation of student,s organisation called her aside, so that the prayer must go on. Before they asked her anything, she told them about her incident. The deligation of student,s saw red and then they told us that she was molested by the thug around the village. Then the cry of horrer rang outfrom, the student,s. Student,s were angry but the dicision was taken by the deligation was to report this metter to the police.

But the right wingers took their own defferent verdict from the deligation. They had gathered themselves next to the gate of the school. so that they could get out of the school yard, to relate the robber, but the gate was locked. They were singing and using bad language so that they could be given the key. lastly they were given the key. They start to hunt the evil person they were led by the raped girl. They looked for him in variety Places that he was accustom to stay in them. In a long run one of the hunters arisen the idea of looking for him in his home. They accept that idea, and they found him smoking dagga, in a spick and span house. They took him while he was amazed. They command him to go with them.

The asked him about the girl that was molested by him but he refused the offence. They arrived with with him in the school yard. He was in tight corner because student,s were armed to the teeth. They ordered him to enter in the classroom but he turned deaf ear to them. In a twinkling of an eye from then the right wingers assaulted him. Those students who were in the classrooms were disturbed by noise. So the had got out of the classrooms to see what was realy happening. The prinsipal had called Police because situation was ungovernable.

In the nick of the time, police arrived at our school, and they were on guard. Right wingers thrown them with the stones. The police warned them using aloud speaker. But they didn,t took any notice from them. The police beguns shotings using rubber bullets and tearsgas. All the right winger,s and student,s they had turned tails. The police played agame because they warned them so that they could save life of the victim. The victim was taken by the police to hospital after he will be taken to the police station to open the rape charge. Unfortunately he died in the hospital because of many wounds on his head.

Teachers told student,s to go home because the situation was not as usual, they did that. Only right wingers left in the school. They were singing and dancing others were smoking dagga. Police return to school so that they could hear more about this senseless killing. Unfortunately they had find only right wingers smoking dagga, the worsen thing theyre uniform was with spots of blood. It was then clear for the police that those lads were the killers. They were in deep water because they were facing two offenses. The were taken to the Police station so that the could be asked the few questions. After that they were sent in to prison the were waiting for appearing in to court. They were regret themselves about the filthy things that they had done.

The folowing day the city news paper abuse the name of our school. By writing with a big alphabets on the front page this "The school of dagga and senseless killings" this heading shocked most of the community. That led to the calling of the head master by the department of education in our villege. The head master was hanged by a thread in the meeting. They were asking him difficult questions at the same time. He asked for short interval because of difficulties in the meeting. Meanwhile he was out, they dicided to close the school and demote him. He return to face his charge,s they told him that the meeting was over. He thought they had forgiven him they didn,t said anything the gave him a letter in a white envelope. He came back to school.

He Pulled his moving seat and sat down. He was down in the mouth mean while he was reading the letter. He called the staff and told them aboat the unfair verdict which was taken by the departament. All the student,s were called in the hall that was unaccustom to be called in the hall. They read a letter to us. The cry of horror rang out because the year was gone for nothing teacher,s lost theire duty that was the pity day in our school. The worsen things are these that chap died for nothing, Our future was spoiled because later we discover that those were lover,s. That girl was the wolf in the sheep,s clothing. Realy that was the day of confusion in our school.

ENGLISH FIRST PAPER
Question 1
Scheme
(1) Education: 1 Par
(2) Life: 2 Par
(3) Future: 3 Par
(4) Family: 4 Par

"I shall remember those happy days for the rest of my life."

As we know that nowadays without education you are nothing and you will end up nowhere. Some people never realised that if you never listen to the teachers advices or parents, it becomes very difficult for one to understand what is exactly going on in education as a whole.

We are people, and we have the right to live according to our expertise and experiences, some of the things that are a hindrence in our lives. Life sometimes becomes more difficult especially if you never went to school or any educational institution, because in life your are faced with a lot of problems, temptations trials and tribulations and those things are the ones that make you feel like commiting suicide, because you dont have any solution to your problems. I believe that in order to live a better life, I must be lively and energetic. Life is what you make it, because whenever you are faced with troubles you dont have to give up easily. I have seen a lot of people being afraid of challenging life as it comes. They start firstly by blaming other people and not considering themselves of what they have done to an extent that life becomes more heavy for them. Preparations in life are there to be made and planned in order that life should not be monotonous and frustrating.

Now that you are growing bigger and bigger as time is passing—by, you realised that you need to plan now and be prepared to have a family, but because people tend to do things differently. My future depends on me and how am I going to handle it. That is whey for me to have brighter and a successful future I must be educated first before I do any other thing. In planning for future is very difficult too as it is without being educated from the beginning of everything. Things that we need to know as people we usually dont take them into consideration, instead we take those that do not involve us at all. We have good examples of teachers, nurses, lawyers, doctors and etcetera of high and professional education, but a few of us will take heed of that education they are havving. So I think that for me to have a brighter future I need to be educated and be able to face life in all the four corners of the world, because sometime to come, we will be living a different life of high qualifications.

A happy family will always show a happy face at all times, because there are people living in that family and they dont regret it for having that kind of a family. They had all the plans for it to be of what it is, because they took their own time and suffered in order for it to be a prosperous family.

In closure I can still emphasize the fact that, if I did not like school, I wont be what I want to be, because these are the days that I will always remember for the rest of my life and I wont be ashamed to tell people of the life I had during my school days.

This paper received a mark of 39 out of 70. The teacher made two red-ink comments: "ADHERE TO INSTRUCTIONS" written across the last two paragraphs in large letters and "Cross your T's properly!!!"

ENGLISH TEST
A day at the Hospital

Early this year when I was still at Mafikeng, I fell sick and my grandmother took me to the hospital. The name of the hospital I was sleeping at is Bobhelong. I was very sick and the doctor have to check me.

When the doctor finished to check me, told my grandmother that they will admitted me. Then my grandmother took my clothes a went back home. Nurses took me to f-3 where I have to sleep.

The told me for not eating anything because at (2:30) half past two I have to go to the theatre where they have to press the cut. Nurse who were admitted me was so kind to me. She looked after me up till at the theatre called me.

At half past two I went to the theatre, then they started to press the cut. They fainted me, I did not saw what they are doing. After that I saw myself again at my ward. I felt that I was now good and there is no pains like other days. I slept there for three days at the fourth the doctor discharged me. Then my sister came to fetch me at the afternoon.

The mark on this paper was 17 out of 40.

[Address and date]

Dear Floyd

Thanks for your letter which I received last month. My friend I am so happy for if you have problems you asked me to advise you. I have heared that you want me to advise for whether you should accept a place at a university. Really I advise you to accept it because when you are at the university, you are going to learn more.

You know that education is important my friend so please accept it. Tomorrow you are going to have a better future. I'll be very happy if you'll take my advise.

I hope you will understand what have said, because it is very important. Please my friend if you have another problem ask me I will help you.

Give my regards to all at home.

Your's sincerely

The mark on this paper was 11 out of 20.

Chapter 12

Week Five

MONDAY

Just Laura, Charles, and a silent student visitor at the afternoon session. Laura is uncertain if I will be able to visit her school on Saturday. There is too much unrest, uncertainty, and violence in Alexandra, where many of her "catch-up" children come from. Last Saturday, they had to get the students back early before the funerals. (Funerals are big community events in the townships, and people get killed at them.)

Earlier, one of the black secretaries told me she has to walk to and from her bus every day past the hostel areas in Alexandra from which the gangs emerge to kill each other and any bystanders who get in the way. Yesterday, gangs of young men arrived in some kind of military trucks and entered houses, firing randomly. Laura is offering to shelter the secretary and her children at her house during the height of the troubles. This is all part of the background to the course, as ever present as the sunshine outside. The daily greetings to Elizabeth, Gertrude, Bonnie, Albert, Brandon, and Benjamin are "Were you all right last night?" and "How is your school?"

Charles and Laura talk about possible outcomes of their seven weeks of effort. Students are still unsure about what authority they will have when they are done, and they think about bringing the staff in this week to help them reach decisions or to "start negotiations."

I point out that the staff are all too ready to join them and to bring the discussions to a conclusion. The staff have some practical problems of their own. They have to organize the rest of the course, allocate instructors and time to it, organize any vacation time they might be able to get, and in general aren't too happy with all the waiting and uncertainty. My recommendation to the group is to invite the staff in during the final week and to have a complete outline of recommendations ready for them. The students should be prepared at that time to explain their recommendations and to tell the staff what they think but not to have the recommendations approved, evaluated, or "negotiated." Details might subsequently be discussed between staff and student representatives, but the crucial time would be the presentation of the student recommendations in the final week, before people started to disperse for vacation.

Charles says that some students would be quite happy to go back to the old system; they would feel more secure. Nevertheless, the experience was worthwhile and should be repeated. Even if the rest of the course was essentially unchanged this year and next year, just going through the experience of having to think about their situation for seven weeks was an essential part of their learning.

TUESDAY

The first of the big work and report sessions, with several conspicuous absentees, like Elizabeth and Gertrude (the prereferendum anxiety in Soweto?), Deirdre, Bonnie, Alice, and Marina. I later discover that Alice and Marina are busy on a word processor, writing up their report for the group.

Laura reminds the group they are getting near the end of the time available for making recommendations and should bring their work to a close. She tells them: "As I understand it, we don't have the final say in what the rest of the course will be like, but we do have tremendous bargaining power if we can come forward as a group. If we don't have a strong consensus, the staff will be very happy to make decisions for us." She says that Charles has set out a list of "options" to see if they all want to follow the same path.

Charles distributes his handout in the form of two columns of seventeen items, with each pair representing extremes on a four-point scale on which students are to express their preferences. The options are:

1.	Product model	Process model
2.	Text based	Discussion based
3.	Staff as lecturers	Staff as resources
4.	Uniform for all	Individual variation
5.	Externally controlled	Internally controlled
6.	Readings as core of course	Readings complementary to course
7.	Staff experience as starting point	Student experiences as starting point

8. Mainly theoretical	Mainly applied
9. Deductive	Inductive
10. Dichotomized	Holistic
11. Answer based	Question based
12. Formal	Informal
13. Mainly lecturer to student	Equal exchanges
14. Course based	Research based
15. Universalized	Particularized
16. General	Context specific
17. Autocratic	Democratic

Charles wants people to select which way they want to go on his list. But he adds that if they are not united—if they are in two groups—perhaps they can argue for alternative Honours courses, the way master's programmes may be divided into research based and practice based.

There is some discussion about Charles's categories. Do people have to vote all down one side or the other? Supposing they like a little of each, like reading and lectures?

Charles: "As I see it, on the left side we will be told what we will study, how to study it, and how we shall be evaluated. On the right side we have a say."

Charles moves on to what a new Honours course should be like: "Although we are a diverse group, everyone here has a teaching focus, so our starting point and our end point must be the classroom. I think it is a wonderful opportunity to say what will be useful to us in the classroom. This is why I have put forward this questionnaire."

There are several suggestions that students would all choose the right side and that staff would all choose the left. Charles says: "If I was a staff member, I'd prefer the right side. It makes teaching more satisfying." He accepts suggestions that he should delete the final autocratic/democratic dimension because it influences all the other judgments.

Mavis, always ready to be engrossed in a task, wants to discuss the individual items on the list. Benjamin agrees.

Charles sees the right side as the path of a butterfly and the left side as the path of a bullet (which is straight and rapid but often misses its target). He throws in the observation that the old Latin grammar still has some uses in the classroom but that he has never found a use for transformational grammar. What is the point of the tree structures that the department is so keen on?

The problem with the university programmes isn't input—there's always lots of that—but intake, says Charles. He has read that trying to learn at university is like trying to drink from a fire hydrant.

Laura thinks it is too late to make choices. At the beginning, they had been offered the right-hand option and had chosen it. Perhaps the group could now make up its mind to continue on that path.

Charles: "Is there someone who could argue for the opposite point of view? Perhaps members of the staff do know far more than we do."

Laura: "Rubbish."

Mavis wants a hearing for the "product" left-hand set of choices: "Why not bring in a staff member to give that point of view? Don't the staff have a role—to mediate, give focus, provide options—while we're swimming around?"

Guy: "Some people might say it's not very kosher to talk about a process model in South Africa at this time."

Mavis (continuing): "We need to find a way around big areas of knowledge. How do you find your own zone of proximal development in this vast sea? You need someone to direct you."

Benjamin: "Need directs you. You go to the other person as a resource."

Charles: "Answers can only come in dialogue."

Mavis (looking at the list again): "What comes first, the lecture or the book?"

Thomas (making a rare contribution): "Don't think that way. Be more task based."

Mavis (persisting): "A student needs a guide."

Charles: "There's room for lectures if we want them. They're just not planned in advance."

Mavis: "There's a problem being part-time. It doesn't give time to think, to explore."

Laura: "There's strength in being part-time. We're not in a vacuum."

Mavis: "There are time problems."

Charles acknowledges the point but adds: "We can work in groups, like the cognition group working on Vygotsky."

Joanna: "There will be areas we don't tap in the process model. We might run into problems at the master's level if we miss something important."

Charles: "But the same applies to the product model."

Joanna agrees. She and Charles have a discussion about terms.

Charles: "Another advantage of a process model is that we can take it back into our schools and continue our own learning. We can continue the course for the rest of our lives."

Laura: "I'm not sure the course was intended to be comprehensive. My feeling is that we've accomplished what we had to do by sticking with it. We've made our choice."

Guy: "The right side would embrace the left."

Laura (pursuing her point): "I can learn things from the group I can't learn from the staff."

Joanna inquires about Thursday: "Are we coming in for group presentations or do we negotiate?" (This term is being used with increasing frequency.)

Laura: "We're going to do what you suggested at the beginning, make presentations to each other."

Joanna: "All of us? It will take all day."

Laura: "Short presentations—five to ten minutes. Fifteen maximum. Do it in an hour."

Brandon, instantly: "Fifteen people for fifteen minutes each doesn't take an hour."

Thomas: "We'll start and see how far we get."

Laura: "There'll be eleven or twelve proposals. We could try to do it all in two hours, then go off and think about it."

Joanna: "We could meet every day."

Brandon: "I can't come Monday."

Charles: "We could have a working group. Anyone who can come could be here." (He will himself be absent all next week, helping to take a mixed group of high school students on a sponsored rail trip around the country.)

Guy: "If we all agree on what we want to do, why have a process model?"

Joanna: "Can't products be generative, moving out from a core?"

Benjamin: "What I studied at university wasn't relevant to me. Now I'm learning a bit, but I'm anxious about the outcome. It's a new road, but I need to walk it."

Brandon needs to know where he's going. He doesn't like uncertainty. Mavis agrees.

There is a general urge to consolidate, and they conclude the class session on that point. But only a few go home; most of them break into their groups.

Brandon pins four large sheets of card on the board. They are covered with diagrams and headed "Constraints on Learning/Teaching ESL." He has ten main categories, with comments on the side. This is his view of what a revised course ought to cover:

1. Psychological climate of learning/teaching (relaxed, inhibiting, concern with "rules")
2. Expectations of teacher ("standards" of English)
3. Material constraints (prescribed textbooks)

   4. Overcrowded classrooms
   5. Social relationships in classrooms
   6. Environmental factors (society, home)
   7. Societal controls (largely political, government/parents)
   8. Cultural issues
   9. Language teaching/learning and ideology (hidden curriculum)
  10. Personal beliefs, ideals.

Brandon explains his display informally to anyone who shows interest.

THURSDAY

Elizabeth comes to the meeting for the first time this week, almost distraught. She says there has been no school since Monday. Despite the
referendum, there has been no halt to the violence in her suburb of
Soweto. "It's continual fighting and killing and dying. Someone threw a
bomb right outside a house—hit a bystander who was then hit by two
police bullets. No one's safe. No one knows when it will stop." She calls
it a "climate of lawlessness." One student had stabbed another because
he hadn't been invited to his birthday party.

The secretary from Alexandra has sometimes not been able to get to
work, and families in her neighbourhood are beginning to abandon their
homes because of the spreading violence among rival gangs of youths.

Against this background, the groups prepare to present their reports
to one another. They come into the room and then disappear. Guy and
Joanna have been tying up the departmental photocopying machine, a
computer, and a printer for two hours—and return to ask me to help
them with a printing glitch. I reluctantly leave. When I get back, Mavis
and Faith have left to do some copying somewhere else. Others go off to
look for them.

Charles sits grimly holding a sheaf of duplicated papers, and Laura
has a roll of blue card in front of her. Impatient because he has to leave
this evening, Charles suggests to the few people in the room that they
might as well go to a pub until they can all get together. This is the
beginning of the "share and consolidate" period he has worked so hard
for, and he is going to miss most of it.

The cognition group—Thomas, Marina, and Alice—arrive like
lawyers ready to present a brief. Laura suggests they start. Thomas distributes a professionally set and printed paper, including footnotes, and
Alice speaks to it. She has the attention of the entire group.

Alice says their recommendation is that the Honours course be a course in language and cognition: "We should study major theorists like Skinner, Chomsky, Piaget, Vygotsky, Luria, and Bruner so that we can intervene in the mother-tongue debate." This is grasping the nettle that I have twice tried to introduce to the staff and have been told it is too sensitive to discuss.

Alice continues: "These theorists all show that for cognitive development, children must have language. Sacks has shown that deaf children who have no access to any kind of language fail to develop an ability to think logically. He says that language opens up the doors of intelligence. Luria has shown that illiterate peasants have difficulty doing certain kinds of things compared with literate peasants. Practical experience cannot compensate for literate modes of thought. On the other hand, Piaget has argued that language is peripheral to cognitive growth. There are wide divisions among the theorists."

Marina interposes: "We need to understand this issue so that we can participate in the language debate."

Alice, emphatically: "We *must* understand it. Mother-tongue education was seen as an apartheid ploy. Now there is a black backlash. They insist on English as a means of breaking into the advantaged world and are prepared to accept the consequences of their decision. Parents and teachers see any delay in introducing English from the beginning of education as part of the campaign to handicap black Africans. We think this would be problematic for black children. It would be unusual for them to be immersed in sufficient English to enable them to learn it as an immediate medium of instruction. Children will find it hard to learn to read in English.

"Zambia has a 'straight for English' policy that gives children nothing but English from six years of age," continues Alice. "When they leave school, they immediately lose any literacy and numeracy they have acquired. There are enormous cognitive consequences for the expectation that non-English-mother-tongue children will be able to do their learning in English. Much of their teaching will be outside their zone of proximal development. It is easy to learn a second language if you have been receiving a good education in your first language. But there are political pressures, so the mother-tongue option may not be viable. We must assume that English will be the main language of government and the economy in South Africa."

Marina (very intent): "In policy discussions and courses, we must go beyond assertions about who wants what. The pressure for English may undermine the natural relation between language and thought."

Joanna: "There is a need to speak standard English. They won't get jobs without it. This is a matter of power."

Alice: "The situation may change in South Africa."

Marina: "Black African may become the standard. It could become the national language."

There is a lively debate on this matter. Brandon reminds the group that all over South Africa, 27 per cent of all black first-year university students fail, primarily because of language difficulties.

The session moves on to the language and power presentation of Joanna and Guy. Joanna begins coyly, telling the group: "We're going to hand our paper out after we've talked because we want to tease you and tempt you."

She and Guy have chosen two specific examples from a dense area of linguistics in order to give a feeling for what it means to explore the area as part of an Honours curriculum. The first part of the presentation is called "What does it mean when you say it?" She hands out a homemade cartoon in two parts showing a manager telling a subordinate to "pull up your socks, man" and then the subordinate telling *his* subordinates to "get on the ball, fix this mess immediately."

She and Guy want to raise the question of whether language represents reality or constructs it, "classifying the world in such a way that it creates the distinctions which result in the speaker looking at the world according to these distinctions." The cartoon is intended to show that context determines whether you see yourself as a top dog or an underdog.

Thus, says Joanna, language is not a mirror but seems to be dependent on the relationships between the addressor and the addressee and their respective social contexts. From this, we deduce that language is social and meaning is social. Language is not static, and meaning is not fixed. This view of the individual and the language used reveals that the individual is not an autonomous, harmonious organism but is continually caught within a variety of subject positions which determines how he or she speaks and what is said. For example, the roles of student and teacher for the same person are often contradictory. Language classifies. When people talk, meaning is constructed between them.

The second part of the presentation is called "You gotta believe it to be it." Joanna acts out a brief rehearsed episode of name calling with Guy and presents a cartoon intended to demonstrate that "sticks and stones may break my bones but words can never harm me" is true only if the words are not taken to heart. Accepting a name results in a surrender of power to the person or situation responsible for the name calling. The idea of name calling can be extended to other areas of language, such as books, when authors attempt to "name call" their readers into a specific subject position.

Joanna says her readings with Guy on language and power fit into the area of sociolinguistics, which has a complex language of its own for classifying and organizing, such as *legitimation, reification, dissimula-*

tion, and *interpellation.* They think the course should explore this area of study because it is likely to make them reconsider what is taken for granted—to make them reflective about language and the way it makes them think about themselves, about their practice as teachers, and about the learners that they encounter. Because it is a complex area of study, they believe it requires mediation by a lecturer who could help them to discover how it could inform their practice.

After all, continues Joanna, what is the point of reading books about a particular subject if we can learn with the assistance of a person in the know? She has heard that we learn from the company we keep. And "company in the know" in this regard would be much appreciated. She explains that the company the group needs is a teacher of semiotics. But they also need reading groups to study particular parts of the area. Words like *hegemony* and *ideology* should be examined. "How do we deconstruct and denaturalize these words?"

Alice says she is confused about what such a course would cover.

Joanna: "We'll have to decide why we want to do it. For example, if our concern is the classroom, what relationships in the classroom are important? We have a reading programme starting with Marx, but we don't feel confident alone in this area. We need to be quite clear on what we need—say, a classroom context—and then study with a teacher. Then we might get the tools to unpack educational policy."

Mavis sees a possible immediate classroom application: "Can we help kids look at texts in different ways? The way language creates bias in newspapers and advertisements, for example?"

Guy and Joanna raise the topic of referendum advertisements and the need to understand the history behind slogans that are being used.

Laura: "All this should be workshopped?"

Joanna: "Yes. You go through a lot of theory to get the practice." She argues for the need for language and power to be studied in school.

Brandon: "I think that what I do in my class lends support to your view. I'm teaching alcohol abuse, and we analyze advertisements to show how they convince people to see themselves in particular ways. We examine the buzzwords like 'new generation' and 'new South Africa.' I always say, 'You are in a jungle and there are animals out there who are fighting for your soul.'"

Joanna reiterates: "Language constructs how you see yourself." Brandon agrees.

Then it is Charles's turn, with very little time left before he must leave. He seems subdued. He has also been somewhat upstaged by the "cognition statement" of Alice, Marina, and Thomas. He wants to take the opposite point of view, as set out in a three-page document that he distributes.

Charles does not believe in starting with theorists. Their conclusions are all disputed by someone else. The group should start with its own experiences, cognitive and affective. The students should develop a list of learning strategies that have worked for them in the past, should use them in the course, and should then go back to their classrooms. "We should pool our strategies. If we find problems, then go to the books."

He calculates that these sharing sessions would take less than three weeks of the year's course, at the beginning and at the end. The debate on whether they should go from experience to reading or from reading to experience (with the guidance of staff) breaks out again.

Alice: "We're battling all the time to get beyond our own experience. We need competing views and understandings of the world."

Charles: "Your reading may take you beyond your ZPD."

Alice: "That's the role of the teacher."

Charles: "You can't expect a teacher to tell you."

Joanna: "The last six weeks have been a pooling of experience."

Charles: "We haven't yet begun to pool our experience."

Joanna: "We've used our experience. Isn't this course about the bridge between theory and practice?"

Charles: "I don't agree. What's the point of having a bridge between experience and a theory?"

Joanna: "How do you know what you want to know before you know it?"

Marina (to Charles, with the debate moving around the room): "We have to move beyond our gut-level reactions to what other people say who've spent their lives on it."

Charles: "Theory is just words that light up your experience."

Guy: "I've had a lot of experience. I want theory."

Charles reiterates: "We haven't started to pool our experience."

Laura conciliates to move things along: "We need to put the two together."

Mavis: "We need the bridge, not one or the other."

Charles appeals: "We should break up into smaller groups to discuss all this."

Thomas (back to the point): "I think theory is embedded in our own teaching."

Marina: "Without theory and other people's contributions, you won't be able to step back from your own experience."

Charles: "But there are contradictions."

Several people: "Of course."

Joanna: "That's lovely."

Charles (warningly to Joanna): "Theorists have power."

Joanna: "Disempower them."

Marina: "You *use* theorists. You deconstruct them."

It's now 5:40 P.M., and the group is pressed for time. There is just one more week to go before they are committed to making their presentations to the staff. There are suggestions that they start meeting every day of the week, but that doesn't work out. As Charles moves rather disconsolately away for his week's absence, the others begin to break up, some resuming their smaller groups.

POINTS FROM CHARLES'S PAPER:

Human cognition is an enormously complicated subject. If we were to attempt to study it from a theoretical perspective, we would devote the rest of the year to it and finally be no better off than when we started. Since our course is an *applied* one, we should avoid this theoretical cul-de-sac and instead pool our own learning experiences, both positive and negative, in order to develop strategies of learning to experience within this course and to facilitate our teaching of our own students. Teaching should be viewed as a research-based activity. The classroom is not a place to apply laboratory findings but to confirm or refute them. This is what the Honours course could do.

The crisis in education in South Africa is often wrongly taken to be mainly a crisis in the schooling system. Since a person who completes twelve years of schooling spends a mere 2.5 per cent of his life in a classroom and since learning is a lifelong process, it seems fair to say that the crisis in education should be seen in a much wider context than the school or university. Our aim as students should be to devise ways of helping our own pupils or students to become effective lifelong learners. A good way to start this would be to pool our own significant learning experiences, both positive and negative. In this way, we will come to consider all the important cognitive factors involved—intellectual, personal, social, affective, and volitional—but in a practical, useful way.

Chapter 13

Preparation

P art of the cumbersome social engineering of apartheid was the establish-ment of "homelands" from which South African blacks were fictitiously supposed to have originated and to which they were required to return if they were not in white employ and not "temporarily resident" in the townships. Although not recognized by any government in the world except South Africa, the homelands were supposed to be fully autonomous self-governing countries, with their own education departments and other social systems. South Africa's responsibilities were limited primarily to "defence" and eco-nomic links.

In contrast to the game reserves, the homelands tend to be the poorest parts of South Africa, lacking mineral resources or land fit for agriculture or livestock. One of the largest, Bophuthatswana, with a population of over two million, is also fragmented into half a dozen disconnected parts near the north central border of South Africa. But "Bop," as the homeland is known for short, is hardly ignored by the neighbouring white population. Taking advantage of liquor licensing laws, tax regulations, and morality codes con-siderably more relaxed than in South Africa, developers have built lavish hotel resorts and casinos in otherwise barren areas of the homeland, together with luxurious condominium estates adjacent to "wildlife parks." All are greatly patronized by visitors from Johannesburg and elsewhere and provide new opportunities for service employment for black Africans.

Income from these enterprises and financial assistance from South Africa have enabled the government of Bophuthatswana to build some impressive public buildings in the capital city of Mmabatho (pronounced *mabatoo),* next to Mafekeng (site of a famous Afrikaner siege of British colonial troops, when it was called Mafeking) and a 200-mile drive through interminable maize plantations from Johannesburg. The suburbs of the capital range from tin shacks to quite elaborate modern homes. I found them reminiscent of Soweto but less crowded and much tidier, with no garbage around, though cattle wandered among the vehicles on the streets.

Amidst the noise and dust of the new construction in Mmabatho (hotels, a convention centre, and a sports stadium) was the University of Bophu-thatswana (known as Unibop), which served as the region's teacher-training institution. The campus was noteworthy for some superior architecture and pleasant open spaces, with much more airy and colourful offices and class-rooms than those at Wits. But despite the conspicuous capital expenditure, current income was low and the university was seriously underequipped and in need of experienced staff, more students, and books and other materials. It was an institution in search of a role, a victim of social as well as geographic isolation. Employment in the "bush colleges" was not greatly desired by aca-demics who could get positions in white South African universities. Yet, it was the kind of institution that had to be strengthened and integrated if South African education was to progress.

A surprise at Unibop was how well the students dressed. They did not wear sneakers and jeans like Wits students (and like their own staff); they wore smart dresses or shirts, ties, and slacks. Some of the staff told me dis-paragingly that students spent money on clothes they should have spent on books. But I was impressed with the sharpness and enthusiasm of the educa-tion students. Many of them had already taught in the schools for years with minimal high school certificates and a diploma and were coming back to "upgrade" to a B.Ed. or B.A. in education.

The college attitude toward students was the one widespread in South Africa: the "deficit" view that black students lacked "information" rather than decent conditions, new opportunities, and a chance to reflect and capi-talize upon the extensive practical experience that many of them had had.

Some staff members quietly complained about government interference with their teaching. I was told later that a former team of instructors had been highly activist and publicly critical of government policies. One by one, they had been dispensed with in favour of more complaisant staff.

SOWETO COLLEGE OF EDUCATION was also a modern and spacious multistory brick establishment serving students who were or would be the DET teachers of the townships. But there were scarcely any students present at the time of my visit. Classes had been suspended following a walkout by students in sol-idarity with ten others who had been denied readmission after failing more than five first-year courses the previous year (a source of contention in many tertiary institutions in South Africa).

The staff of the college—mixed black and white—were friendly and receptive, though most of them found concepts like whole language difficult: "Teachers should be eclectic, but they can't give up control. I read to my children, but they don't read voluntarily. They are good readers because of the spelling lessons they were given." There was great confusion over spelling and phonics: "How can children identify words they don't recognize if they don't know C is pronounced sea?" But that is scarcely unique to South Africa.

Because of the violence in Soweto, college staff cannot take their students into schools for internships, which makes the student teaching even more textbook dominated.

There was also violence at DET colleges of education in rural areas. At one college of education, white lecturers were attacked and the buildings burned down. A lecturer died after being set on fire. Black students blamed frustration over white domination of the training institutions, the DET closed down several colleges, and anger and bitterness increased.

> LANGUAGE POLICY NEEDS to be as fair as possible to all the languages. This would need to be shown by supporting the development of indigenous languages so that they can more easily be used as teaching languages.
>
> The issue of languages in this country often appears to be very problematic to South Africans. We created this problem ourselves. It is therefore up to us in the area of education at least, to build an educational language policy which, in the final event, works equally to the advantage of all South African pupils. (Macdonald & Burroughs, 1991, p. 73)

Over 25 per cent of black children drop out of school before the end of standard 3 (grade 5); the year English becomes the medium of instruction. According to the ANC, those who complete school often do so with little respect for indigenous languages. Black students who graduate into public service professions such as medicine, education, and law often cannot communicate with their patients and clients because they do not have a common language.

"The way to achieve high levels of bilingual proficiency is to promote the development of the minority language—the non-dominant, non-prestige language—in school" (Cummins & Swain, 1986, p. xvii).

Krashen (1991b) summarizes research showing that students learn "considerable amounts" of second language, as well as "impressive amounts" of subject matter like mathematics and history, when the focus of the class is on the subject matter being made comprehensible rather than on the language.

In a survey of education in Pacific Island schools, where English usually becomes the medium of instruction in the third or fourth year, Elley (1991) says:

> In contrast to students learning by means of structured, audiolingual programs, those children who are exposed to an extensive range of high-inter-

est illustrated story books, and encouraged to read and share them, are consistently found to learn the target language more quickly. When immersed in meaningful text, without tight controls of syntax and vocabulary, children appear to learn the language incidentally, and to develop a positive attitude toward books. In some cases, the benefits are found to spread to other subjects and languages. (p. 375)

There have been suggestions in South Africa that what might be best socially and economically for black adults in the long run might not be best for children currently in school. McLean (1991) commented that the achievement of a nonracial educational system might require language policies that are unsatisfactory in the classroom ("a mild form of oppression") and to the advantage only of those already most advantaged in South Africa.

ABOUT TWENTY WITS STUDENTS, black and white, made afternoon visits to Soweto to help black children with their reading and writing. A black official of the National Educational Crisis Committee (NECC) told the group the problem was not with black education but with education generally. NECC was against the separation of black education and white education. For years, whites had been taught they were superior to blacks and blacks were taught they were inferior to whites. Any government must attend to this. There were great disparities between black and white educational contexts. One had libraries and laboratories; the other didn't.

But the government was beginning to see a different scenario, said the speaker. The education crisis was being felt by every section of the population. The white birth rate was falling. White teachers were being laid off. White schools were being privatized. On the other hand, the townships needed teachers. The authority of teachers must be restored. In the past, the only way teaching could take place was through corporal punishment. Now that that threat had been removed, the teacher's authority had been eroded. It had to be restored in some way.

But some of the black Wits students told me that many DET teachers still beat their children, sometimes specifically and sometimes randomly as a group punishment. Children thought this was natural; they would do it themselves. But the custom should not be regarded as traditional. Kallaway (1984) attributes the "intense recourse to corporal punishment" to the high failure rates that followed the 1976 breakdown of education in the townships.

AT THE LUNCHTIME MEETING, an instructor from the education department admitted to once having shared the common South African view that black students lacked certain essential experiences or skills. If these could be topped up, they would be all right. But after reading Feuerstein and Vygotsky, the instructor decided the students suffered from a lack of mediated learning experiences; the problem was not with the students but with their "reality."

"To understand these students," the instructor continued, "examine their meanings, not their behaviour. Don't try to change minds; change realities. ASP students [black students in the university's academic support programme] come into university thinking it is the same as their own spaces of activity—that the new is the same as the old. We must learn why there is a mismatch between meaning systems. For these students, there is no historical continuity with what they bring. Feedback at the end of courses comes too late to construct new meanings."

A colleague said a strong black "culture of education" existed before Bantu education, but it had only been for an elite at missionary schools, where people like Nelson Mandela and Archbishop Tutu were taught English. After the student boycotts in the 1970s, they "couldn't get kids back into schools." Teachers had been relatively untrained and were poor role models in English. And now the whole system had collapsed.

Another staff member said that when children had been learning in their mother tongue—under official Bantu Education until the mid-1970s—their instruction was defective and resources inadequate. But this staff member was now adamant that "the time for questions is over, and right or wrong, we must start rebuilding, not destroying." This meant concentrating on English.

THE CONCERN WITH HIGH FAILURE RATES among black first-year students at Wits was occasionally tied to the realization that many of their textbooks in all subjects might be incomprehensible to them. Their grasp of English and of subject matter might be weak, but their textbooks might also be poorly written.

Nevertheless, most students went or were sent into the Wits academic support programme because their written work was not up to scratch. An instructor in the programme told me they understood that massive correction might interfere with learning to write, but they nevertheless felt students had to produce writing so that errors could be corrected. If students couldn't write, how could anyone tell what they didn't know?

Critics of academic support programmes said they were band-aids and paternalistic, treated students as if they were intellectually deficient, and stigmatized students among their peers. They also made more work for students who already had to work harder than everyone else. There was a trend in many centres toward using academic support expertise to teach course instructors rather than students and to provide support in subject areas rather than English skills. But everywhere there was a lack of resources for programmes without formal academic content, which depended primarily on corporate and individual donors.

It was not just writing that many black students found alien about university, but everything: the emphasis on time, the general busyness, and the arcane cachet that came with the possession of "knowledge." Literacy was another vehicle by which authority was exercised; it was not a source of enlightenment or even entertainment but the locus of control.

Literacy was a regime, and as in any regime, different people had different degrees of authority. Literacy did not help the disenfranchised to learn; it dictated what they were expected to learn. It was an obstacle, not a goal.

A BLACK INSTRUCTOR AT WITS had a demanding, unsentimental attitude toward black students: "He's a malingerer," "He's no good," "She's a failure." This polyglot instructor refused to speak anything but English with black students—"This is an English language university"—and reprimanded a black student who remained seated during a brief conversation with me as I passed by: "Stand up when you're talking to the professor."

THERE WAS TO BE A "STAY AWAY" IN ALEXANDRA as part of a campaign to close the migrant-worker hostels, source of most of the violence. This involved everyone staying home from work for the day, a most effective tactic—especially if Soweto was also involved—because Johannesburg would lose its maids, maintenance workers, and general labourers.

More than a hundred people had been injured in clashes with police as crowds of local residents tried to march on a disputed migrant hostel. A Wits secretary was anxious because she had sent her children to school in the morning, when it was quiet, but would have trouble getting them back safely through the streets again in the afternoon.

There were different kinds of demonstrations in downtown Johannesburg, where thousands turned out for a ticker-tape parade to welcome home the returning cricket team. Politicians told them they had enabled South Africans to hold their heads high with pride throughout the world again and reestablished South Africa as a nation.

Chapter 14

Week Six

MONDAY

To my surprise, no one turns up for the class: an empty room. This is "independent working time," of course, but I wonder for one last time what has happened to all the resolution of the previous Thursday and if all the group members really are working.

Joanna arrives half an hour later, just as I am about to leave. She is concerned about the course again. She doesn't think "process" is the answer and fears the group is going round in circles. Nevertheless, she has lost sleep and abandoned her social life thinking about the course. Once again, it is mainly the others she worries about: They need direction. She thinks that language and power should "inform" the whole course. Otherwise, people "in the know" should teach them what is considered relevant.

TUESDAY

Elizabeth and Gertrude are absent again, raising concern about the situation in the black schools; also absent are Charles (on his train trip) and Thomas (undergoing eye surgery).

Mavis makes a businesslike beginning. She pins a sheet of newsprint on the board, with large rough circles on the left and right labelled "theory" and "practice," connected by a bold blue double-headed horizontal arrow, with batches of smaller arrows and explanatory writing all around. At the bottom is a colourful drawing of a large fire-breathing dragon on a field of question marks: the "grammar dragon." The topic her group has chosen is "the skills"—by which they mean reading, writing, talking, and listening—with a focus on "real classroom stuff."

Mavis says her group decided to first look at theory and then move to practice. But they realized that a double-ended arrow was required, moving between theory and practice. "Where do we start?" she asks. There are many constraints on practice (which Brandon will discuss). And the question of the grammar dragon always comes up: Should we teach grammar?

"How do children learn to read?" Mavis asks rhetorically. "What is the role of . . . " and in an arresting demonstration of the utility of phonics, she adds a word that she pronounces *phone-ics.*

Several voices: "What?" Guy: "Do you mean phonetics?" Alice emphatically: "*Phonics.*" Mavis returns to the diagram.

Mavis: "First, we should examine the general picture, then move to the more concrete. Our proposal for course discussions is to start with our own practice, then move to drawing out our private implicit teaching theories, then compare these theories with current expert theories."

She is asked how practice might change as a result of exposure to theories. By informed criticism of practice, she says. Possibly they could design new materials, do research, and publish. She gives an example. Before she started studying theories of reading, she thought that meaning was in the text. The questions she asked were based on Bloom's taxonomy, with lower, middle, and higher order skills. Now she has encountered theories that readers *make* meaning out of texts. This will lead her to forge a different approach to reading and comprehension activities.

Albert quietly steps in to help. He pins up on another wall a smaller diagram on crisp pink card, with multiple arrows in coloured inks. (I note a contrast between the diagrams the students have been making and those the staff produce when discussing courses. The student diagrams are full of circles surrounded by arrows, looking like battle plans. The staff diagrams tend to be grids or boxes, looking like barricades.)

Albert explains: "This is what I think Mavis had in mind in a different way. We start with our current practice in skills teaching, indicated by the circle on the left of my diagram, then move with this arrow to compare our own theory with expert theories." He continues round the clock to show how practice can be modified and become the beginning of a new cycle.

Mavis resumes: "I also did something on writing and materials. I wanted to motivate spending some time discussing materials and perhaps developing some materials in the course." She reiterates her view that "new ideas" introduced through contemporary materials, with teachers' notes, could be "helpful." She proposes a debate on whether materials disempower teachers. "Can teachers be trusted?" she asks.

There are some conversations around the room on these issues. Then Mavis continues: "We could critically look at some textbooks and alternative materials and then go on to develop materials of our own if we think it useful. Materials could help teachers get to understand the potential of students and would therefore be empowering to teachers and to students. Literally millions are being poured into materials development in South Africa. It has been found that teachers don't know how to use books, and most of the money now goes into materials."

Joanna: "If teachers are dependent on materials, there's a reason for it. It's a consequence of teachers being disempowered during their training."

Mavis, who trains teachers, agrees. Mavis says she had been most impressed by a presentation she had heard Joanna and Guy make last year demonstrating materials they had themselves produced for rural work.

Joanna: "You empower first, then get on to materials."

Mavis hands out some duplicated notes and says: "I want to say something about writing as well. We think there are many important relationships—like writing and thinking, writing and speaking, and writing and teaching—which are usually very structured. How useful are the different approaches? And again, there is the grammar dragon."

Joanna: "There's an enormous focus on grammar in the recent English curriculum in the United Kingdom. It has a horrifying effect on teachers and high school students."

Deirdre: "We should discuss the constraints on materials production, like time and money."

BRANDON HAS BEEN STRUGGLING to get an overhead projector working and appeals for help, supplied by Guy. He peers at the group through his thick glasses, flashes his wide smile, and makes his presentation:

"We decided that I should look at constraints on ESL teaching. I looked for them in my own teaching and other people's. I made a very long list. I went into a class—the students wanted to talk and I wanted to teach—and I realized that I was a constraint myself.

"Perhaps it would help if I described my own background and experience. I come from a society that has been oppressed, exploited, and deprived, and education has been used to maintain the status quo. Language teaching has been used to promote the interests of the oppressors; it comprises a dominant part of the curriculum. Three of the six matriculation subjects are languages [English, Afrikaans, and a vernacular]. At Wits, there is a debate going on since the mid-eighties that the university is elitist, Eurocentric, and irrelevant to most people in the country. This is where I come from. These experiences influence what I want to learn.

"I'm also a teacher at the secondary level. When I first began teaching, I was given a textbook to use, a mark schedule to record, and told to send any problem to the office. It's a very rigid and boring way of teaching, but we do it for the sake of passing exams.

"We must reflect on what is happening in South Africa. We are going through drastic and rapid change. All sections of the population are having problems coping with the change. But with these changes, there are implications for education. The question is how prepared we shall be. I have some proposals. Our focus as language teachers must be on difficult areas. We are under pressure to do this. Students pass exams, but they can't use language effectively in society and in their jobs."

Joanna: "In DET schools?"

Brandon and Guy: "Everywhere."

Brandon (who struggles with overheads while he talks): "The question is what is the goal of teaching ESL? What do we want to achieve? I think the aim must be to *use* language effectively in all areas of society, not only to pass exams. I can propose several ways to deal with the constraints.

"First, we should teach students to think within language, teaching language as a tool to work with in society in a practical way. Second, I try to teach how language as a whole is put together—not small bits of language, but how information is organized in language and how language is used. Self-expression demands confidence, and I want confidence training in language use. Students must be able to use language assertively.

"My third proposal concerns overcrowding in classrooms. There is an impression that black kids are invading white schools. But black kids by reason of politics and history have always been in large classes. In just one class, I must teach English to seventy-two students. Teaching at Wits is based on the assumption that teaching is in a class of normal size. I was taught no strategies for overcrowded classrooms. I followed what my teacher did to pass the exams. There's a lot to learn about the teaching of large classes. There should be research. The problem will be with us for a long time.

"My next proposal concerns language and ideology."

Joanna: "Yeah, great."

Brandon continues: "Language is never free of ideology, and there's a lot of ideological language involved in the changing South Africa. We should study these matters.

"Finally, I want to pick up on a point of Mavis's. We all have implicit theories of language teaching. In my five years' experience, I've always been interested in what my colleagues do. We all seem to have implicit ideas. We put aside our university training and develop our own unconscious beliefs. These need to be unravelled. We must literally "see" how they inform our practice."

Guy and Joanna applaud. Brandon goes on to explain: "I meet people in business and industry who say, 'You're teaching English? What are you doing in your classroom? The kids can't use English.'"

Guy: "Why do you let them criticise your classroom? Maybe what's wrong has something to do with the private sector that criticises you. How much control do their institutions have over the individuals who work for them? You're sending your students into a sausage factory."

Many small conversations break out. Guy, who wears loose casual clothes and rimless glasses, with his fair hair in a pigtail, adds: "I'm an anarchist, and no one will listen to me."

Joanna: "The system is responsible. They practise apartheid education, and teachers get blamed. It's not enough to give students the language of the marketplace; the oppression will continue. We must empower them, so they can read critically the texts that oppress them."

Guy: "English isn't my first language. [It is Afrikaans.] Now I speak this institutional language, and thereby I support and maintain it. I learn so I can say 'Ja baas' [Yes, boss]—that's using language effectively."

Mavis: "Aren't there two questions here: politics and ideology, and teaching effectively?"

Several: "They can't be separated."

The class is constantly in motion. We sit in a room just big enough for the eighteen of us, with long tables round three sides, facing the door and the chalkboard. When the students are in their groups, they cluster around individual tables, but in the class sessions, they sit against the walls. Heads and bodies turn in unison toward the person who is speaking. This movement becomes quite lively and balletic when the exchanges are rapid.

Laura comments: "Because of the way we teach, with the emphasis on grammar and correctness, students aren't empowered."

Benjamin: "Students in rural classrooms only experience the language in school. Textbooks aren't working. We need to find an alternative."

Guy: "You're trying to teach kids to go out and be understood. But what's wrong is outside the classroom. You're maintaining the situation outside. It's a vicious circle."

Laura muses: "Pedagogy is always ideological if it is prescribed." The discussion becomes general again.

Joanna: "In 1976, mother-tongue instruction was resisted. What's the position now in black schools?"

Albert: "People thought that if English was introduced earlier to children, they would learn it earlier. But some of the experts say that you should develop their own language for the achievement of cognitive abilities. In rural schools, they just don't get enough English. So, why try to teach it?"

Joanna: "Children are told they need English to get jobs."

Laura: "Their parents, grandparents, and schools tell them that."

Albert: "The ANC wants all languages upgraded."

There are recollections of events in the 1970s, the student boycotts, and the mother tongue versus Afrikaans dispute.

Marina: "The power lies in the English language. It's the language of imperialism and capitalism."

Alice: "You speak English because it gives you power."

Guy: "I only *think* I have power, but I don't. I'm playing into the system."

Brandon: "I've heard it said that writers must write in their own language and that subjects like biology should be taught in Zulu. But others say do away with vernaculars; they are outdated and useless."

Guy talks of the rejection of Afrikaans: "If Afrikaans can't make it in modern South African society, what African language can?"

Laura, passionately: "It's very hurtful for anyone to be told that their language is irrelevant or outmoded. If I was told that, I would feel outraged. To deny a person's language is to deny the very essence of them. It worries me when I hear black people say their own language has insufficient value. It indicates how indoctrinated they are."

Brandon: "Some parents punish children for not speaking English."

Mavis: "Workers in the coloured areas may be speaking English and Afrikaans equally, but they see Afrikaans being swamped. They're sorry, but they want their children to learn English."

Eleanor: "In my school, there is a large Portuguese population, and the parents wouldn't give up their language. The parents insist that the children learn Portuguese and speak it at home."

Faith: "Chinese schools don't do that. As a little girl, I pushed my own language aside. Later, I wanted to go back and learn it. It's probably better to leave vernacular language learning to later."

Guy: "Why not earlier?"

Laura: "Because children don't see the relevance of it."

Mavis: "What does all this mean for this course?"

Guy: "It's very serious. This course should be called Applied Language Studies, not Applied English Language Studies."

Albert: "That's right. Look at all the other languages we speak here. I'm a Xhosa speaker."

Brandon: "English is our focus, but we are looking at other languages."

Laura: "Aren't we all English teachers? We'll all continue teaching English. So, Applied English Language Studies is addressing what it means to teach that."

Benjamin: "I teach English between 6:00 and 8:00 P.M. and Zulu from 8:00 to 10:00. I have more trouble teaching Zulu than English because I have to teach Zulu *through* English. So, I have to use the word 'adjective' in talking about Zulu, although Zulu doesn't have adjectives."

Albert: "That is power."

Laura and Mavis look at their watches and express concern about getting the reports completed. Everyone has been absorbed in these conversations.

Mavis wants the presentations to continue on Wednesday and Monday (the two afternoons that have been devoted to individual activities): "There'll be a need to consolidate and organize once the presentations are made. We've got to start talking about strategy; we've got consensus on content, but how should it be put together in a course?"

Joanna and Laura agree. The recommendations must be ready for the staff next week. There are suggestions about working at nights and working through the weekend. No floundering now. And as we leave, an excited Joanna tells me how worthwhile it is; she is glad I hadn't accepted her pessimism yesterday.

POINTS FROM MAVIS'S HANDOUT:

Good teachers can be trusted to discriminate between good and bad materials, and materials can in fact have an empowering effect on teachers by introducing them to new ideas and encouraging experimentation. The following issues should be explored: Do materials create dependence in teachers on outside "experts"? Do they manipulate pupils and teachers into accepting dominant ideologies and cultures? Do preformulated, structured materials limit teachers' own creative responsiveness to their own pupils' needs?

A great deal of money is currently being spent on materials in South Africa. In whose interests are these materials produced, and who benefits? The publishers? The materials writers? The students? The teachers? The educational authorities? Those in power? Those who wish to change society?

How can we compensate for the lack of educational opportunities and enormous backlogs in South Africa without new materials and new textbooks? How can teachers with minimal training and language competence themselves be expected to manage independently? Is the problem more concerned with teacher education? Is massive in-service training of teachers affordable? Are materials a more effective "way in" to change? What is the importance of spelling, grammar, and punctuation? At what stage in the writing process should we attend to errors? Society demands correct writing. This puts teachers in the middle in that they need to "nourish" their students, as well as meet the demands of society. Do teachers need intricate knowledge of grammar in order to understand student errors? How can teachers assess the linguistic resources of their pupils and establish what structures they need to be able to perform communicative activities?

THURSDAY

A slow start for the last scheduled meeting of the Honours group before the final week, with Charles, Elizabeth, Alice, Brandon, Benjamin, and Thomas absent and several others delayed for a variety of reasons. Only half a dozen are present at the beginning, impatient to get started. Gertrude, who has been sick, and Bonnie are busy on the department copying machine. Laura comes in ten minutes late and is surprised that the others haven't begun. Marina wants to start planning the proposed outline of the course, but Laura points out that presentations are still to be made. Everyone has to be heard. Time is short, and discussions with the staff are to begin next week. Laura suggests "one-minute presentations." Marina thinks that while they wait for others to come, they should brainstorm about how the presentation to the staff should be made. Laura acquiesces reluctantly.

Joanna enthusiastically heads to the board, and an immediate misunderstanding ensues. She chalks a huge schematic umbrella—which she calls a *spray*—across the top of the board, with a handle down the centre and three numbered rectangles across the bottom indicating the three remaining quarters of the year to be organized. Laura and Marina ask what she is doing. "Planning the rest of the course," she explains. They think they are planning the next four days. While they are debating what exactly they were planning, more people come in and Joanna is left stranded as the others quickly move on to the rest of the presentations.

Deirdre, whose turn comes first, is not to be hurried. Although there are still arguments about how the afternoon's time is to be organized, she explains that her topic was the impact of first language on second-language learning and hands out photocopies of quotations from six different sources. Her particular concern is: "What is the right age to teach English to black children: preschool or later? What will language policies be in South Africa?" Everyone sits quietly but not conspicuously patiently while she takes her time going into the theories of the six authorities she has cited. "Is language learning different from learning other things?" she wants to know.

One of her authorities has reported that foreign students enroled in regular courses at the University of Hawaii did as well without supplementary ESL instruction as other students who received supplementary

instruction. "Thus, the evidence is that ESL instruction makes no difference," says Deirdre, "so why teach ESL?" She continues with her own
lengthy case study of a group of newcomers to South Africa who learned
English at different times at different ages in different ways. Her conclusion is that age is not relevant in language learning if motivation is strong
enough. *"Affect,"* she says, "is what learning is all about."

Laura takes this opportunity to begin her own presentation. She
thinks there is a huge field of study in affective factors theory related to
second language learning, both inside and outside the classroom. What
are the effects of risking danger to come to school and of encountering
riots and even death on the way to school? Is there any way second-language learning experience can be used to assuage student emotions? She
thinks teachers get a lot of feedback about how students are handling
second-language learning cognitively but nothing about the emotional
consequences. They know when students fail, but not why. Affective factors probably play a bigger role than they are given credit for.

Guy: "Wouldn't taking all these factors into account intimidate the
classroom teacher even more?"

Laura: "We shouldn't just go on preconceived ideas. We should be
ready for anything."

Bonnie is concerned with sociocultural factors in second-language
learning. She says: "I don't have an idea of English culture myself. The
reason I hate Afrikaans today is because of culture shock in school. People aren't willing to withdraw from their own culture into another for language learning. Teachers should address themselves to feelings of failure,
frustration and anger."

For the skills group, Gertrude has compiled a list of questions about
spoken language. For example, should spoken language be taught or just
be part of everyday activity in the classroom? Should they have "oral
periods" and just speak? How long should students be expected to speak,
on what topics, and who decides this? As teachers have to give marks,
who should get the most: the child who speaks the most or the one who
provokes the most discussion? Should marks be given for fluency or
accuracy? Children love to act—should drama be part of the language
classroom?

Gertrude's concern as a teacher is whether she is leaving anything
out. She would love to give vocabulary drill but knows this "is not
encouraged." Translating into mother tongue is the easiest to mark, but
should they do so much of it? It is difficult to set aside time in the classroom for just talk, and the inspector comes along and wants to see what
work they've been doing. These are all practical matters the course
should address.

Guy, Marina, and Albert think there has been enough discussion, and Joanna and Laura want to get on with planning. Joanna, who has been waiting near the board, finishes drawing her umbrella. Under one section, she writes "thought and language—theories."

Marina wants consideration of the status of English in South Africa and its usefulness. Several discussions break out.

Marina says: "Africa is a multilingual continent, yet we are trying to impose English; how do you explain this?"

Joanna adds "language and power" to the board and then "English hegemony."

Joanna wants advice on how much theory could go into the class-room: "This question comes up all over." She also adds "dialect and reg-ister"—"there are problems here" and moves on to "strategies." More dis-cussions erupt, and Joanna archly objects to "conversations in the group" while she is working at the board.

Marina proposes adding "discourse analysis"—how do people talk to each other? Joanna offers an answer: "You analyze the way people speak, and you draw out the relations of language and power, make it less theoretical."

Mavis wants "core areas" to be added and spread out all over.

Laura: "All the areas will spread out."

Mavis: "There's the theory and practice issue, like thinking and learn-ing. It's all tied in with teaching methodology and the grammar dragon. Testing comes into it."

Joanna: "Everything comes into it."

Mavis: "There are the classroom constraints, like large classes. And the materials debate."

Guy: "That's related to power—institutional versus teachers."

Albert: "When we're talking about communicative competence, we're actually talking about grammar. Are we saying students have to learn this? We want students to communicate, not learn grammar."

Joanna: "No. It informs our teaching."

Albert: "Grammar is problematic. Our group isn't sure about its rele-vance."

Guy: "Grammar books are being prepared for South Africa in which the grammar is implicit. They're great fun."

Laura: "Can one only learn implicitly or can you learn explicitly, deliberately?

Mavis: "The question is how much grammar we consciously need to know to learn a language."

Laura: "Enormous amounts of grammar are taught, but very little learned."

There are fifteen minutes left. Joanna invites the group to "sum up"—

and then to decide what to do with what she has put on the board. But they are losing Marina, who has become impatient with the failure to get on to the presentation to staff. Gertrude also leaves. The others begin a debate about what the umbrella represents: second-language learning or just language learning?

Mavis: "It's not just about language acquisition. It's about use and the nature of language."

Deirdre wants her "biological factors" included, such as age.

Joanna: "Biological age or cognitive age?"

Deirdre: "What's the difference? I'm concerned with the optimal age."

Deirdre, Laura, and Joanna begin debating how to get everything on the board, seemingly indifferent to the time. Joanna waves her hand authoritatively across the tangle of arrows and labels on the board and asks: "Is anyone getting this down so we can photocopy it and circulate it?"

She is asked: "To whom? The staff?"

Joanna: "No. To the students."

Mavis, decisively: "Then we've got to work on the weekend."

Arguments suddenly break out about whether motivation is part of affect. Joanna is trying to find a place to include every topic or issue that anyone mentions. They are now looking for any buzzwords they can think of, such as "culture shock" and "communicative competence."

Eleanor: "Communicative competence should be a category of its own, but it fits into many other things."

Faith adds: "It would be interesting to look at interlanguage and error analysis." There is a discussion about where those would fit in. The chalk flies fast in these last few minutes.

Joanna: "So, next time we should regroup all this?"

Guy: "How is this plan different from what we had before from the staff?"

Joanna: "Should there be a difference?" There is some tension between Joanna and Guy at this point.

Guy, emphatically: "A big difference."

Deirdre, perhaps reminded of what the staff might have wanted, asks whether anyone wanted to get phonology in. She and Joanna debate its placement on the crowded board.

Mavis, to Guy: "This is much more classroom based and experience based than the old one."

Guy: "It looks the same to me."

Laura, the facilitator: "There are more options. We're not looking at lectures on all these things but at how we find out about them."

Guy: "I can handle that."

Mavis: "There could be some lectures."

Laura: "The whole thing is practice oriented."

Guy (preparing to leave): "It doesn't look like it to me."

Joanna, stepping back to survey her elaborate diagram like a proud artist: "This spray is the outcome of our seven weeks' work."

Albert, softly: "The question now is what we do with it."

Mavis: "We start with our own practice—with skills, for example; we write papers; we use it as a basis for drawing out our implicit theories." Some of the group start to leave.

Joanna persists: "We need to take the spray and regroup it into priorities. It's not content oriented."

Laura: "I see it as options. We can't all do everything."

Mavis: "Core and options."

Joanna likes this suggestion and returns to the board with chalk ready: "So, now what's in the core, and what's in options?"

Guy pauses on his way out: "Why a lecture model?"

Laura: "Brandon said he was lectured to for a year and never learned anything."

Guy said he would settle for talks, workshops, discussions, or reading groups—but not lectures.

Laura: "We must establish an agenda and control the questions. Different people must take responsibilities. We can't do it all."

Suddenly, everyone realizes that they are almost at the end of the day—and of the preparatory week. There are scattered conversations about how the work can be completed in time for the presentation to the staff.

Mavis impulsively becomes organizational and says: "Is this clear? We come in tomorrow at 2:30, Saturday at 2:30, and Sunday at 10:00."

There is rapid discussion about getting in touch with absent group members and organizing entry into the university during the weekend.

FRIDAY

I have other university commitments and join the group ninety minutes after they start, to find five of them working intently. Brandon has come in from the country at only a few hours' notice. Faith has diligently prepared and distributed a neat version of Joanna's spray board, and Guy has returned in a more buoyant and collaborative mood. Mavis is as staunch as ever, and Laura declares: "We've got so much work done. We're really getting organized." She adds thoughtfully: "I hope the others go along with this."

Guy, confidently: "They will."

They have "identified four themes" that could be spread over the remaining three quarters of the year's course. The themes are:

1. Language learning
2. Language and thought
3. Skills (the stuff of the classroom, says Mavis)
4. Grammar.

These are areas in which questions could be raised and explored by "options groups," like reading groups and study sessions, which would "float around" the main topics.

Guy: "It's like a tree. The themes are the main branches and the questions shoot out from them."

Mavis explains the approach for "skills": "We'll follow Charles's suggestion and start off the first session reflecting on our own experience of learning, with some written preparation for all of us. This discussion won't be pursued but will remain as a background for everything that follows. Then for the next couple of sessions, we'll prepare specific papers on how we teach reading, writing, talking, and listening. We'll unravel our implicit theories, which will become the main focus of the sessions."

Laura: "We'll spend a minimum of time on presentations and a maximum on discussions. The staff can suggest readings."

Faith says she doesn't like the kinds of "reading packs" the staff usually provide.

Laura: "It's okay if you have a choice."

They want the staff to attend as "facilitators" not "teachers." Their role will be to help the group think, not to tell them what to learn. They propose that there should be two staff facilitators at every session to present alternative "expert" points of view. The staff participation should be "collegial." Then the students will revert to discussions of practice in their own classrooms.

Laura: "We're all teachers here—except Faith, and she'll become one. The beginning of all these sessions will be our classrooms, and the end will be our classrooms, too. Practice will be the topic of all our papers."

They decide that it will not be necessary to spell out in detail how time will be allocated to each theme, although the first one will be given as an example. The structure should remain flexible, and periods will always be held in reserve for independent or spontaneous activities. They should do a lot of writing and should consider working collaboratively for publication.

They give some thought to evaluation. They recognize that the staff might not be free to follow all the student proposals, and they examine the university requirements. They are ready to accept that there will be a final mark and that university requirements are that at least 50 per cent come from examinations. In previous years, this has been on the basis of

30 per cent for a final examination and 20 per cent for a research project or dissertation. The other 50 per cent, they think, should probably come from a couple of major pieces of work rather than being parcelled out over a large number of "course work" presentations and assignments. (In the previous year, the final mark was calculated as a percentage of a total of 1,800 marks allocated to examinations and other parts of the course.)

But they want to suggest different possibilities for some of the evaluation at least: for oral presentations, collaborative work, and materials written for publication.

SATURDAY

Faith, Laura, Mavis, Brandon, and Joanna arrive promptly to meet in my office. Joanna gives me a symbolic present: a package of *laager* tea. Faith brings a package of Chinese cookies. Joanna is part of the morning group of six full-time students that is beginning to feel very special, and she wants their part of the course to continue independently. But the part-time students want to see the morning sessions as part of the whole.

The session then begins with explanations to Joanna about what was done yesterday. She circles items on her copy of the spray diagram to see what has been "covered." She then wants to discuss options and how they will be evaluated.

Laura and Joanna have a dialogue about "oral examinations." Joanna says that the group discussions had been wholly against the notion of "expertise." Do they now want students to be exposed to examinations by panels of experts? Brandon describes his own wretched experiences of trying to making himself clear to university faculty.

Joanna: "The entire class could give a mark—or at least have their opinion count half and half with the staff."

Laura: "The staff might ask if we don't trust them—or they might not trust the students." She sees no point in examinations at the Honours level. But she and Mavis want to come up with some solid proposals about evaluation or they will be told what to do.

Mavis, matter-of-factly: "Evaluation is useless. Teachers always know whether students have learned. Supposing we all do different things?"

Brandon: "In my school, students miss tests and get sent to the subject teacher, who can give them a mark as well as any test. The teacher can look at a student and say, 'This is a 50 or a 60.'"

Laura: "We're only getting evaluated because the university wants it. That's a lousy reason."

Joanna: "A degree gives you access and has to be based on evaluation."

There is a lively discussion about "who decides who fails."

Guy arrives, and they realize time is passing. They get to work on the themes, elaborating the titles. At Mavis's suggestion, "skills" becomes "the stuff of the classroom." Because of the vagueness of "language and learning," this topic is modified to "relations between language competence and specific learning tasks," with a rider reflecting the evaluation discussion: "the key role of writing."

They spend the rest of the time spelling out the timetabling of the first theme, emphasizing two "critical factors":

1. The themes should be classroom based, beginning with personal experience, bringing out "implicit theories," contrasting these with "expert theories," and moving forward to modified practice.
2. Staff should work as facilitators rather than as teachers. Two facilitators should be present at every session to represent alternative points of view.

The group allocates twelve sessions of the forthcoming second quarter to the "skills (the stuff of the classroom)" theme, specifying a topic and a procedure for every session. They become concerned that they will not have the time to achieve this degree of detail for the remaining three themes but decide that it would be sufficient to spell out just the first theme "as an example" and to make the point that they want to be flexible about the entire year in any case.

This time, for the first time, they get the conclusions of their discussions on paper as a draft for the written presentation to the staff, using the office computer. The afternoon ends with a continuation of the discussion about the need to study "grammar."

SUNDAY

A prompt start again, with a slightly different cast of characters: Mavis and Laura, Joanna and Guy, Deirdre, and—back from his train travels—Charles. They began once again with a discussion about the morning sessions for full-time students. Charles is informed that this matter has been "sorted out."

Albert, Faith, and Gertrude (after her long drive from north of Pretoria) arrive, and the furniture has to be shifted around to accommodate the group in the small office. Mavis has brought fruit juice, plastic glasses, and biscuits, and others have brought their own coffee mugs. They are all thoroughly at home.

Once again, the opportunity is taken to revise what has already been decided upon in explaining everything to those not present the previous day. When the idea of providing options is raised, Joanna wants to be organized and says: "We'll have to make a list of them." She is still concerned about including everything that is on her spray.

Laura says an advance list of options will not be necessary: "They'll arise."

But Mavis has also prepared a list. She never gets to present it, though she suggests some additions to Joanna's list. It is pointed out that for staffing considerations, the university discourages more than four options in a course. They decide that their list, already twice that long, could be called "study groups." Joanna changes her heading to read "options/study groups."

The evaluation debate is resumed. Laura asks Gertrude, Albert, and Brandon what they think about written examinations that favour students whose mother tongue is English.

Albert is opposed to writing in order to be evaluated: "That's why we're against exams. They're confusing and frightening and don't really address our ability."

Brandon (quoting): "They're an insult to our intelligence."

Gertrude: "Oral is better. You can explain misunderstandings and clarify."

Joanna tends to favour examinations. "They make students focus." She has spent intensive periods studying books and acquiring knowledge, which she would not have done without the motivation of an examination.

Mavis suggests that if there have to be examinations, they should be based on fifteen-minute presentations that students make to one another, distilling what they as individuals have learned in the course. Examination content should not be restricted to what the examiners want.

The topic switches to the evaluation of course work. Deirdre wants to include "problem solving." They all lean over Joanna as she tries to write out a scheme for marking. There is a debate on the relative roles of staff and students. Laura reasserts the teaching experience and expertise of everyone round the table. Mavis still likes to think the staff have expertise. The discussion moves to the concept of "competence."

Albert: "Who decides whether students are competent?"

Laura (firmly): "Us."

Albert: "Students should have a say. But how do we do this?"

Charles suggests a simple pass-fail on each theme: "This would not be competitive." Albert likes this.

Mavis: "We need marks. You need 65 to go on to a master's in this university."

Deirdre wants to know what happened to the university system of first-, second-, and third-class pass levels.

But Mavis has been thinking about Joanna's remarks and now talks of the value of preparing for examinations.

Guy: "We can't avoid competition—it makes a difference in the university whether you get 64 or 66. But we could make it broader."

Laura: "People fall into three categories: incompetent, competent, and ready for the next step."

There is a long discussion about the concept of competence and the relative allocation of marks.

Laura (suddenly): "Look at us. We're students designing a course and deciding how to evaluate it. That's an enormous task we're accomplishing."

Charles: "It takes some people years."

Mavis (getting them back to earth): "So, we want evaluation but not exams."

There is agreement, but then they go back to how the 30 per cent would be allocated to the examination.

Laura likes presentations to panels in which the panel raises topics.

Guy: "That's interrogation and manipulation."

Brandon wants consultation on the limits of the examinable material.

The discussion of mechanics continues. There is a concern with the notion of group work. Some people—like Gertrude and the absent Benjamin—live a long way away.

Brandon wants rehearsals for examination presentations. He is again concerned about competition and says the students should support one another.

There is a digression when Deirdre unexpectedly asks me why I am not staying in the country; I have begun to talk individually with the students about reaching this decision. We briefly discuss whether the situation in South Africa is unique. I point out that teachers in bilingual education and ESL have worked in violent situations in Los Angeles, Detroit, and many other U.S. cities and in Britain, South America, and many other areas of tension, sensitivity, and severe social and political constraint.

Brandon: "South Africa needs to be left alone for a while."

Albert: "We've been left alone too long."

Brandon: "We must get our own house in order first."

Albert: "Whose house *is* in order?"

Charles: "Why can't we just forget we're South African?"

The group returns to the business at hand and resumes discussing how the presentation to my staff colleagues will be made—how much written and how much verbal. It is agreed that Joanna and Brandon will jointly make the opening presentations, with Charles in the chair. I shall not be seen as being on either side.

They adjourn after three hours for the final meeting of students tomorrow, which not everyone will be able to attend. The plan is for a first formal meeting with the staff on Tuesday, an unplanned day for students on Wednesday while the staff reflect on their response, and a concluding meeting of students and staff on Thursday, the last day of the seven weeks.

Chapter 15

Alternatives

The almost complete breakdown of Bantu education in South Africa after the student boycotts led to the establishment of many fly-by-night shop-front schools. Anyone could put up a shingle and claim to be an educational institution. Considerable profit could be made from black parents anxious to find education for their children. A few of the alternative schools had become established and reputable. I visited one in a white Johannesburg suburb; it was so reputable that Wits sometimes sent education students there for training internships.

The 250 students were all girls, black, and about fourteen years old. They were friendly, collaborative, articulate—and lucky. Many had received little education in the past, but they were now better off than the great majority of their peers. They arrived in the morning in a fleet of black taxis, which returned to the school in the afternoon to take them back downtown, from where they would take buses or taxis to their township homes. Their parents were mainly domestic workers, often single mothers, who paid Rand 280 (about U.S. $140) a month each for one, two, or even three children to attend. They valued education highly, but they also wanted their daughters sheltered; life was harsh for young girls in the mixed township schools.

The alternative school had been opened on a small hand-to-mouth scale by three women who, like many white South African teachers, felt compelled to do something to help young black South Africans get an education. Their efforts were so successful that they were able to gain institutional support from one of the large South African mining corporations to rent an old convent, a more attractive site than even many white schools. They could afford to pay teachers above standard and could be selective. They chose young and adaptable white teachers, but classroom activities were still very structured and unimaginative—something I found in all the schools I visited. The head teacher said that she wanted new ideas and that she recognized the school had a long way to go.

I saw one teacher opening a "book club" for her English class, a good idea she had read about. She brought in a supply of new paperback books from which each student was to select one (for which parents would be billed). There could have been a good deal of student reading, writing, and discussion about the books, but the students actually did nothing during the entire period and the books stayed on the teacher's desk. The teacher summarized each book's contents, and the students raised their hands if they thought they might be interested in getting it at the end of the period.

Another teacher spent a period teaching "family relationships" like "father," "sister," and "uncle" with photocopied illustrations of white faces with European names—to black students for whom relational terms like "uncle" had familiar but totally different cultural connotations.

The performance of a young black student teacher—a product of teacher training at Wits—was embarrassing to onlookers. She was loud, strident, and authoritarian, marching up and down the rows of desks and rapping them with a stick to emphasize her points. She was trying to teach English by requiring students to underline all the past-tense verbs on scraps of dimly photocopied text, ruining any story there might have been and committing a number of unnoticed errors herself. I was told her style was "typical black teaching" and was often the best Wits could do with the best of black candidates for teaching degrees. The students were not particularly attentive to her. I was also told that black students did not think they could learn English from black teachers.

To me, the problem of black teachers was no different from that of most white teachers: a complete lack of opportunity to see or learn what schools could be like outside the harsh and rigid confines of South Africa.

DEIRDRE'S SCHOOL HAD A SIMILAR HISTORY. Established by a white mathematics teacher in a warehouse near Soweto in 1986 in response to appeals from township parents, it had grown into a coeducational high school with twenty teachers for nearly 300 black students aged from fourteen to "mature." The government had recently agreed to release some unused white school buildings for black education, and after a number of moves the school was now for the first time accommodated in premises actually built for educational purposes, with properly equipped classrooms, laboratories, and a library. The students were matriculating at four times the rate of students in regular DET schools, and the school was beginning to expand into community college activities. In acknowledgement of the school's contribution, the DET did make a small grant, but most of the funds had to come from donations, fees, and fund-raising events.

THE "OUTREACH" PROJECT that Laura had initiated was in its third year. It was one of several similar projects that had been started, although funding sources were beginning to dry up. It brought about a hundred promising black students from Alexandra to a tranquil and well-equipped white suburban school building for four hours on Saturday and two hours at the end of the regular school day, two afternoons a week. There, they were helped to prepare for entry into "open" white schools, where white parents had voted to accept the admission of a small proportion of black students, perhaps 10 per cent. The project also seconded a teacher to two DET schools in Alexandra so that the teachers and students there would have an opportunity of working with a "mother-tongue English speaker." It was also arranging informal meetings between DET teachers and teachers in the white system so that at least some could get to know one another.

Ten Alexandra schools were invited to send ten of their best students aged from eight to fourteen to Laura's project, where they were given a battery of creativity and aptitude tests and only taken on if the staff felt they had a reasonable chance of getting into and succeeding in "open schools." The majority of the students who took and passed the entrance examinations for the project and for the open schools were girls. The project was having a difficult time with students unable to concentrate because of violence around their homes. Students came to the project for a period of three or four years, after which they were helped to take the admissions examinations for open schools. But staff still found it necessary to stay for an additional year with those who succeeded. The leap from a DET school culture to a white one was enormous.

There were no crowded classrooms at the project, which had a staff of half a dozen classroom teachers, including a young black African male and a young woman from the United States. There were also sports coaches and a social worker to help the students adjust to white schools. Because black students found it so difficult to feel comfortable in a white environment, the project paid particular attention to nonacademic activities like swimming and tennis, which white students would probably be accustomed to and black students almost certainly would not. The students were also given extensive opportunities to gain experience on computers and "to think."

Students were getting the experience of working more intensively in small classes with white teachers in a mainly white environment. The classroom activities were more representative than exemplary. In one class, seventeen eight-year-olds were copying mathematics exercises from the board and filling in the blanks in a workbook. In their English workbooks, they had been doing exercises on apostrophes and prepositions. They had been divided into "butterflies and grasshoppers" according to ability. They sat on the floor to hear a story, with a preponderance of teacher talk and preparation. The teacher had chosen a story popular in the United States, with a farm setting that was not exactly familiar to the children, but several were clearly entranced by it. Older students in another class were starting journals, though the free writing I saw was limited, and Laura was introducing a senior group to the idea of writing and publishing a class magazine.

I was told that most white teachers in the open schools were unprepared for the change to accommodate black students and needed long-term support themselves, which did not exist. Many were actually frightened by the prospect of teaching black students. Apartheid had been a success in separating black and white; they were only just beginning to try to get together. White schools needed to change, and there was also a need to change the admission tests, which were poor indicators of how black students would be able to settle into the open schools. Black Honours students had earlier told me they still felt white culture to be very alien. Obviously, fluency in English does not automatically make black students feel comfortable or accepted in English-speaking environments.

BLOODSHED IN THE TOWNSHIPS CONTINUED. It was so commonplace that newspaper editors must have wondered whether there was any point in reporting it issue after issue—as I wonder about reiterating the blunt fact of violence in every other chapter of this book. But these were the conditions in which South Africans were living, working, and teaching; they were the background to the Honours students' deliberations.

Some students were with me in my office when the secretary from Alexandra came in early and distraught. There had been shooting all night, and her family had had no rest. She had taken her children to school because they would be safer there, and she had come in to the university for the same reason. Her husband had stayed home to protect their house.

Mothers in Alexandra had appealed for security for their homes around the migrant hostel, but more shots were fired and people injured. Zulu residents of the hostels were allegedly trying to drive the nearby Xhosa residents out of their homes in order to occupy them, and the ANC was allegedly sending in retaliatory groups to attack the hostel residents. But many injuries suffered in the previous days came from baton blows, rubber bullets, and bird shot—all police weapons—as well as from pistol shots.

Leaders of the ANC and the Inkatha Freedom Party made eloquent nonpartisan calls for peace. This was not the way to go into the future, killing each other, they said. The police complained that both the ANC and the Inkatha Freedom Party were blaming them for inciting or encouraging the violence. The air was thick with claims and counterclaims—all in fluent English.

ACCORDING TO NEWSPAPER REPORTS, British educationist George Walker, director-general of the International School in Geneva, told a Johannesburg conference that the challenge for South Africa was to develop a new system of education rather than try to move toward the system used in white schools. He said white education was "impoverished in scope and authoritarian in approach . . . towards regurgitation, not towards open-ended skills-oriented education which would give graduates the flexibility to deal with the uncertainty of the future."

ALBERT WAS RELENTLESS in blaming teachers for the state of black education in South Africa. They were passively trying to teach in a language they did not understand, but they felt threatened if they were called upon to talk about the situation. He could not get teachers into study groups because of their anxieties. They were not well trained themselves; it was a self-perpetuating system.

There was a desperate lack of facilities, but the fault was still with teachers, who would not speak up sufficiently. Students got inadequate educational experience, both in and out of school. They wanted recognition and understanding, not teachers endlessly talking at them. Students rebelled, and teachers were often assaulted. Teachers were also often challenged by students, who wanted them to be more progressive and politically relevant.

Brandon said that political pressures were not so strong outside urban areas. People still believed in education. The "culture of learning" was not a universal problem in South Africa. The basic problems in his school were shortages of textbooks and other facilities. They were also overcrowded, with some classes having over seventy students. Brandon used "democratic methods," but the school still had corporal punishment.

Many teachers at Brandon's school were graduates, including the principal. But Albert said the right people did not often come along looking for teaching jobs in Soweto. Most teachers had only a diploma. His first priority would be to take apart the colleges of education and restructure them. The key was to get everyone in education interested in change.

BRANDON HAD FAILED TWICE in his first year at school. His mother was told there was something wrong with his brain.

ANY STUDENT WHO FAILS the final Honours examination at Wits is forbidden to write the examination again anywhere in South Africa for ten years.

Chapter 16

Week Seven

MONDAY

In the morning, Elizabeth calls to explain why she missed the weekend's meetings. Violence has decreased in their area, students have been returning to school, and they all have to be tested to make up for the marks they have missed in preparation for the exams. The inspectorate is also coming this week, so she is not sure about getting free for the presentations, though she will try.

At the afternoon session, Laura, Mavis, Albert, Brandon, Charles, Guy, Joanna, Deirdre, and Faith prepare and rehearse the oral presentations to be made to the staff tomorrow. They ask me to act as devil's advocate for the staff, but I decline.

They first glance through the draft of the recommendations they have prepared. There are some anxieties and second thoughts. Charles, who missed most of the original discussions, wants explanations of the themes. They all sound the same to him. What does "alternative descriptions of language" mean? Grammar. What does "the relationship between language competence and specific learning tasks" mean? Grammar. Shouldn't they have a separate section on grammar? Grammar is everywhere. Laura suggests actually putting it in as "the grammar dragon." This idea is rejected, but theme four is made specifically grammar almost all the way through, starting with the basic issues: "Should grammar be taught?" and "Which grammar?" (Charles adds: "I don't want to be doing trees all the time.")

The Document

The final recommendations presented to the staff at the Tuesday meeting were in the following form:

GENERAL OUTLINE OF PROPOSED HONOURS COURSE
_____

Four core themes (plus options)—each theme with two facilitators
representing different points of view. (Each theme will consist of 12
to 14 sessions—2 sessions per week—plus one session for options.
Dates to be decided.)

Theme 1. Language skills (reading, writing, listening, speaking—"The
          stuff of the classroom")
Theme 2. Nonlinguistic factors influencing language learning
Theme 3. The relationship between language competence and specific
          learning tasks
Theme 4. Alternative descriptions of language

All themes will follow the pattern of moving from personal experience to expert theory, discussion, integration, and forward to modified practice. Preliminary reading lists should be generated by students and the two facilitators together at the beginning of each
core.
   The following detailed outline is provided as an *example* of the
treatment of all themes.

THEME 1: LANGUAGE SKILLS (READING, WRITING, LISTENING, SPEAKING) ("THE STUFF OF THE CLASSROOM")

  1.   Group's language learning experiences
 2.–5.   Implicit theories (on reading, writing, listening, and speaking)
 6.–9.   Expert theory (arising from 2–5, leading to a revised reading list)
10., 11. Politics of skills teaching. Constraints
12., 13. Specific evaluation and testing skills—same cycle of personal
          experience, discussion, and controversies
14.   General discussion (back to practice with new insights)

(continued on page 156)

THEME 2: NONLINGUISTIC FACTORS INFLUENCING LANGUAGE LEARNING

1. Intrinsic factors (age, nutrition, motivation, anxiety . . .)
2. Interpersonal factors (roles of parents, peers, teachers . . .)
3. Sociopolitical constraints (language and power, language policy)

All the above considerations permeate classroom practice. The treatment of the theme and its distribution over sessions would be similar to that for Theme 1.

THEME 3: THE RELATIONSHIP BETWEEN LANGUAGE COMPETENCE AND SPECIFIC LEARNING TASKS

- With a critical analysis of the key role of writing, as a means of learning and of thinking, and as the primary means by which learning is evaluated
- The mother-tongue debate
- Multilingual classrooms

The focus of this theme, as with all the others, will be from the classroom point of view, looking at intrinsic, interpersonal, and sociopolitical factors. A similar cycle of inquiry will also be involved, moving from experience and implicit theories to expert theories and discussions of modification of practice.

THEME 4: ALTERNATIVE DESCRIPTIONS OF LANGUAGE

Should grammar be taught? Which grammar?

The relation between teachers' knowledge of grammar and student learning:
  Part A—relation of grammar to discourse and critical language awareness
  Part B—relation of grammar to classroom practice and ability to communicate effectively

Possible options or work-group topics: materials research and development, role of teacher as facilitator/mediator, whole language, multilingual classrooms, media in the classroom, etc.

PROPOSALS FOR COURSE EVALUATION

20 per cent: *Dissertation*—assessed by staff, to be made available to and read by students.

30 per cent: *Examination* (alternative to written examination):

1. 15 per cent. Student choice of oral or written presentation in which students individually consolidate the year's work in a comprehensive framework. The presentation should be made to and evaluated by all students and staff, so that the group will benefit from each other's learning.

    and

2. 15 per cent. An oral forum in which students are engaged in debates in specific subject areas, with smaller staff/student groups who will do the evaluation.

50 per cent: *"Course work"*—selected from a variety of alternatives, including: individual and group papers portfolios of writing, classroom demonstrations, individual or jointly authored papers for publication, and presentations by individuals and groups.

Recommended: In place of marks, the following categories:
*   Doesn't graduate
*   Graduates
*   Graduates ready to proceed to higher degree work

[The document concluded with detailed
timetabling recommendations.]

TUESDAY

Presentation day. The students are dressed more formally than usual, arrive promptly, and seat themselves around the room to leave spaces for the staff, who arrive tardily. Most of my colleagues sit together in a phalanx near the door. The dean also arrives and sits close to the other staff, more relaxed than anyone else. For once, I do not sit with the students or the staff but find a corner, confining myself to note taking.

There is no response to Charles's welcome from a silent, unsmiling staff. Then he invites Laura to describe the first quarter of the course.

Laura: "The past seven weeks have been an enormous challenge but a valuable learning experience. The task was enormously difficult, daunting to some, emotionally taxing on our motivation and sense of purpose, filling all of us at times with confusion, frustration, and even despondency. But we persevered and made progress, and today we are confident about the proposal that we have to present to you. We are a diverse group, but the fact that we are all teachers has given us a common background and purpose. Teaching has been our focus throughout, and we have built our experience into our proposal.

"We have already benefited and learned a fair amount from each other. Taking responsibility for this part of the course has made us more serious about it than if it all had just been given to us. We feel valued. Some of us feel more serious about issues outside the classroom as a result of this experience.

"We have learned from each other in our discussions, and we look forward to learning from the staff in a similar way. Rather than formal lectures with content set down in advance, we see our sessions in terms of workshops and discussions, facilitative, collaborative, and exploratory with the staff as facilitators and colleagues, with their own kind of special knowledge that we can benefit from."

The staff sit without comment.

Confidently, smiling Brandon then describes the process leading up to the formulation of the proposal: "We began with brainstorming and open discussions, sharing our experiences and our own conceptions of language. We then split into small groups to identify and focus on specific issues. We drew information from a variety of sources. Schools were visited, we referred to academic books and to individual staff, and we drew a lot from each others' experience. Then we reported back to the class as a whole on what we had done, either as smaller groups or as individuals working alone.

"These report-back sessions were characterized by critical debate. We then tried to put the pieces of the jigsaw together to represent the views of the class. We also critically examined the evaluation system.

"Our proposals, if they are accepted, will require changes and adjustments by students and by staff. There must be a will to experiment with new ways of learning and teaching. If that can't be done at the university level, where can it be done?"

Then Joanna, regal in an embroidered purple velvet high-necked jacket, releases the copies of the four-page document to be circulated around the room and "walks through it," reading every line of the text aloud, inviting questions (but the staff are too busy reading), and adding occasional brief explanations.

After going through the evaluation sections, Joanna adds: "The idea is to create a cooperative rather than a competitive model of learning."

The staff do not respond.

Joanna says: "That's it."

The staff are busy reading, making notes on their copies of the documents and making quiet comments to one another.

Then the response begins. There are no thanks, no acknowledgements, few observations, but many questions that are blunt, forceful, and to the point. It is like an oral examination.

Staff member 1, pointing to the document: "Who evaluates the course work?"

Joanna: "That's open to negotiation."

Staff member 1: "What are these portfolios of writing? Are they essays?"

Joanna: "People have been writing from the beginning of the year. Anything that contributes to the course or in the field can go into the portfolio."

Mavis adds: "The idea is that not everyone should write on the same topic."

Staff member 2: "I don't know how the fail, pass, and pass with merit scheme will fit into the university's way of doing things. If your proposal is accepted, none of you will be able to get funded in the future. The funding bodies start at the top with marks and work down."

There is more silence, which Charles breaks: "The students have had seven weeks to prepare this document, and the staff have only had it for seven minutes. Perhaps we should give them more time."

But the staff want to continue.

Staff member 2: "Why two facilitators? Do members of the staff have that much power? Can't the group itself present different points of view?"

Joanna: "It's not a question of power. The staff have expert views. We want to hear what the differences are."

Staff member 2 (missing the point): "I've always enjoyed team teaching, myself."

Staff member 1, pointedly, indicating the document: "Who did this, staff [meaning me] or students? Honest answer!"

Joanna: "There was some consultation in some groups, but many worked without assistance. On the whole, the staff respectfully kept their distance."

Staff member 3: "This is a summary of a whole term of thinking. It would be nice to know what is *behind* these recommendations. Do students themselves know enough for this kind of course?"

Joanna: "The second quarter is given to acquiring knowledge and the third quarter for application."

Staff member 3: "Take us through that. I don't follow."

Mavis: "We see it as a dialogue, starting out with our own ideas and knowledge, using that as a bouncing board for encountering expert theory."

Staff member 3, indicating the theme regarding alternative theories of language: "What do you propose in here? You can't do Halliday in one session. The staff themselves have a study group that has been working on Halliday for weeks. What makes you think you can do him in one session?"

Joanna, conciliatory again: "We have a possible split built in here. Students could select which route to take."

Staff member 4 backs up the questioner: "If you want to look at Halliday, you need to apply his whole theory. It can't be done in two or three sessions."

Joanna (gives up on this one): "Good point."

Charles: "We see it as a debate."

Staff member 3 changes tack: "Does anyone here, for example, understand the definite article in English? That is an important matter if you're teaching English to Zulu students. They don't have articles in their language. How would you explain the article in English to them?"

Guy: "That will come out of our experience."

Staff member 3 persists: "If the answer to my question [about understanding the definite article] is no, then teachers *need* grammar. They can't teach English unless they understand the grammar of the article. Where will you get that information?"

Joanna: "How long do you need?"

Staff member 5: "The discovery method is uneconomical for this kind of study."

Several students, reiterating: "How long?"

Staff member 3: "You could do a Ph.D. dissertation on the definite article."

Charles, trying to find a way out: "The process we're proposing is designed to lead to learning how to learn. The initial reading lists would be revised, and students would look for leadership."

Staff member 3: "That stuff's hard—you can't do it with individual study. We told you that a group of staff has been struggling with Halliday."

Staff member 5: "And it can't be done by consultation."

Charles: "We know how to use study groups. We do it at our schools."

Staff member 3, sadly: "It's really very difficult. It takes a lot of time."

Charles: "If the staff has so much difficulty with Halliday, is there any point in trying to relate it to the classroom?"

Mavis: "Our whole focus has been on the classroom."

Staff member 6 changes the subject: "Where is first- and second-language acquisition?" Students indicate several places in the document, and the staff member nods.

Staff member 4 tells the students there should be a lot of flexibility so the staff could express their own interests and expertise.

Joanna: "There are the options."

Staff member 3 returns with a new point of attack: "In theme 3, what are these 'specific learning tasks'?"

Joanna struggles: "It's how much language you need to learn particular things—it's the chicken-and-egg problem. It's 'cognition.'" She asks Alice to explain.

Alice, a little surprised but quickly picking up: "We looked at how the topic of language and cognition was tied up with the mother-tongue debate [whether black students should be taught in their mother tongue or in English]. We wanted to consider alternative approaches."

Joanna: "That's what theme 3 is about."

Staff member 7, sitting beside Joanna and making extensive notes, interjects sharply: "Could I ask how you arrived at the decision to give equal time to all these themes? If it's a coincidence that the themes each group came up with all happened to need the same amount of time devoted to them, then it is a remarkable one."

Joanna is disconcerted and has to be reminded by other students that there was a good deal of shifting around of specific topics after the group reports were made before the content of the themes was finally decided upon.

Marina unexpectedly indicates she might be ready to cross the floor, with an observation that does not come from the student discussions: "We looked at our own experience of teaching, formulated questions, and then we looked for our own solutions. But we didn't know what we needed to know. I didn't know that a course on phonology might help me understand why African students made spelling mistakes. I think we should welcome advice."

Mavis, holding fast: "This is for debate."

Staff member 1 makes the first positive comment on the document: "Pretty good product; very good." Staff member 6 nods agreement.

Alice, picking up on Marina's comment: "We are coming up against the limitations of our own experience."

Staff member 8 wants a rationale for having two facilitators in a two-hour session.

Laura repeats: "To provide alternative expert points of view."

Staff member 2: "You must have a wonderful faith in staff members to expect them to produce spontaneously exactly what is needed. How can they prepare?"

Laura: "That would begin to surface right from the beginning. Facilitators would be getting direction from the group."

Staff member 2: "That's unrealistic. Staff always need time to prepare."

Laura: "Wouldn't facilitators choose themes about which they'd already be prepared?"

Staff member 6 suggests closure: "This is a proposal. The staff will study it, and then we'll jointly negotiate. Then we'll come to an understanding of what we as the staff consider relevant."

Joanna, packing up her papers: "That's a very nice proposal. Logistically, how shall we negotiate this? We could come back a week early next term."

Laura, firmly: "The staff meet tomorrow. We negotiate on Thursday. Is any more time needed?"

Charles: "We don't want to put the onus on the staff—we want to work it out together."

Staff member 3, tight-lipped: "I know this is an unpopular view in some quarters, but the job of a facilitator is to structure access so that you don't all start at different places. You can start at a difficult place or an easy place, but that requires a properly sequenced course."

Mavis, doggedly: "It must be trial and error. We can't plan an entire course the way it was before. This is a mutual challenge."

Staff member 1: "The staff could express their own interests?"

Charles: "These could be part of an option or part of the core."

Staff member 3: "I'm talking off the top of my head, but I can conceive that it would be better to start with new knowledge rather than experience. Is that acceptable? How fixed are you?"

Mavis, coming back again: "I don't think anything's fixed, except the idea that all learning must start from what you know. You move in cycles."

Staff member 4: "The starting point could be anywhere."

Alice: "We need to hear the staff's responses, not push everything into options."

Staff member 6: "If we're in negotiation, we need to know how flexible you are. Staff may want to throw things out. How would you react to that? What's your commitment?"

Joanna protests: "It's unfair to ask a question like that. We need the whole picture."

Laura: "Remember where we come from. We've all got quite a lot of experience—and, therefore, quite a lot of questions. That's why we're here in the course. That's the one thing we feel strongly about—we want to go back better equipped, with more insight. That's how I see it."

The staff are immobile and silent. Staff member 3 fires a final salvo: "One thing worries me a little bit. In preparing the document, you've lost the questions that gave rise to it. I don't really know what your questions are."

Charles: "We're looking for opportunities to raise questions. Someone has said we aren't what we eat, but what we digest. We don't want a lot of knowledge thrown at us that we can't digest."

Staff member 6: "This is a methodological question—I see it in terms of negotiation."

Staff member 3 sets an assignment: "While the staff are meeting, give us a list of your questions so that we can understand your thinking."

Charles, reflectively: "That could be valuable."

The tenor of the meeting changes at this point. The staff have given the students something to do, and the students' attention turns to how they will do it. The staff are in control.

Staff member 6: "I suggest we stop now and give you all an opportunity to get your list of questions in."

Staff member 7 asks how the students will get their questions to the staff and requests that some students stay on hand for "consultation" at the staff meeting tomorrow.

Deirdre: "Will there be a collection point?"

Charles: "So, I guess it's all over."

Guy: "I want to reiterate that it will be us and the staff, not top-down. We should keep that it mind."

Staff member 7, firmly: "You're assuming everyone thinks that top-down is wrong and learner-centred is right. I don't."

Guy: "It was what the group felt."

Staff member 7: "Yes, I know. It's wrong."

ONLY STAFF MEMBER 3 remains for any length of time to chat with students, and that is to reiterate a point: The list of questions was required so that staff could understand the students' thinking. This is challenged by Brandon, who thinks that the questions are an unnecessary assignment. Why can't the staff accept the student proposals and respond with their own ideas?

Students afterwards stand around, saying they feel flat. Laura thinks the staff were challenged and felt insecure. The situation was difficult for them. Joanna thinks that the staff are acting like staff and that the students should probably do what they want. Albert in his quiet way is the most outraged. He thinks the staff were not listening to the students and simply wanted to defend their positions. Guy believes it was part of the "academic game."

WEDNESDAY

As the staff meeting begins, I am told there is a crisis. Staff member 3 and staff member 1 are looking grim. Staff member 7 is rigid and soon reveals a furious anger. I place myself at the side of the long table, but the others sit so that I am facing them all. I feel on trial.

Staff member 7 reads forcefully from a prepared statement: "There are several useful questions in the student document, but language learning and teaching are complex and cannot be dealt with in such an order. As proposed, the syllabus is uninformed and unrealistic. It is a disaster. There should be an investigation of the past seven weeks. They have been a catastrophe, a complete waste of time. The staff will have to clean up the mess."

Staff members 1 and 3 say they support all this and have concerns of their own.

I ask if staff member 7 would read the response to the students. "Certainly." Staff member 3 says they should do it as a group; the staff are in it together.

I suggest that the staff have been attacking the document in too much detail, looking for weaknesses from their own point of view rather than trying to hear the student voice behind it.

Staff member 5 agrees that too much attention is being given to the wording of the proposal and asks why staff member 7 thinks it is uninformed.

Staff member 7: "For example, they've given two sessions to testing and evaluation when we normally give fourteen. There's nothing for phonology, and I don't see where psycholinguistics fits in. I don't see how to start a course with methodology. There seems to be a totally inappropriate allocation of time on the nonlinguistic factors theme."

Staff member 3: "I agree. There's far too little."

Staff member 7: "I think there's too much."

Staff member 7 continues: "The thinking's muddled. Look at theme 3—a focus can't be a point of view. The theme 3 emphasis on the key role of writing should be in theme 1. And there's no acknowledgement that grammar means the grammar of sentences. As a programme, I think it's nonsense. It's a complete waste of time."

Staff member 1: "The students were given something they've never been asked to do in their lives. They could have done it in two sessions. I don't think the document's bad. It was thrown at them. They did their best."

Staff member 3: "There's no sense of history in the document. It suggests that you can't learn from the experience of others."

Staff member 4: "I'm very uneasy about the whole experiment. It's very unfair to the staff. Not all teachers teach in the same way."

Staff member 7 bursts in again: "I'm appalled. It's an ignorant mess."

Staff member 5 tries again: "But we do have an attitude to the document. We're judging the document with such intensity, complete and utter dismissal, when we should be thinking of our relation to the students."

Staff member 7: "Students are *not* experienced."

I respond: "They've been teaching for years at Soweto and other places."

Staff member 7: "They're not experienced at the Honours level."

Staff member 3: "They must have phonology."

I reply to staff members 3 and 7: "Why do you look at me all the time? I'm not responsible for the document."

Staff member 7: "Of course you are."

I continue: "I was responsible for the course, but the document was written by the students."

Staff member 7, very angry: "You were responsible."

I reply: "Would you find it easier to continue this discussion if I wasn't here?"

Staff members 3 and 7: "Yes!"

THURSDAY

In the morning, staff member 7 sends a memo to all the staff and delivers a copy to me. It says: "I am deeply committed to our work and try to oppose, within my ability, anything that I believe to be an obstacle to it. . . . I will continue to oppose what I believe to be obstacles to our work."

Staff member 7 is also concerned that I take notes during meetings, though it is a customary academic practice.

THE FINAL SESSION OF THE HONOURS COURSE is a well-dressed occasion, with several of us formally dressed for a graduation ceremony elsewhere in the university later in the afternoon. Faith is graduating at the event, and so is Laura's daughter.

My colleagues tell me they have decided that staff member 4 should preside over the proceedings and should present the department's "offer" to the students. I say I would like to make a few remarks of farewell before passing the group over to the staff for the rest of the year. This is dubiously discussed and given uneasy approval.

Not a great turnout of students. Joanna had said she would be absent, and so are Brandon, Elizabeth, and three or four others, so there are almost as many staff present as students.

I speak briefly. It has been a privilege working with the group, I have learned so much, they have produced a fine document, and I now hand the course back to the staff.

Staff member 4, in businesslike fashion, tells the students that the staff have discovered many ways in which their interests can be fitted into the student framework. They propose looking only at the second quarter this afternoon, leaving the remainder of the course to be considered later. The general feeling among the staff is that the students' proposed outline was drawn up from the perspective of the classroom teacher. This was more appropriate to an education course than to one in applied linguistics [sic]. The course should be broader. So, while respecting student interests, they feel they can bring a lot to enrich the student point of view. Besides, many students will go on to do other things than teaching—they will do research or get a higher degree—so again the course should be broader.

Then the matter of the two facilitators: It is a wonderful idea. Many of the staff are doing it already. The only problem is that it is somewhat impractical. The staff are already stretched. They can't do it on an everyday basis, but they will do it whenever they can. They also feel the document lacks a sense of history: There is no developmental perspective. The course should look at how an individual and society evolve in linguistic terms.

Staff member 4 draws a second-quarter timetable on the board. For full-time students in the morning, "option 1" on Mondays, "language learning and teaching" on Tuesdays, and "dissertation work" on Thursdays. For part-time and full-time students in the afternoon, theme 4 ("alternative descriptions of language) on Mondays and the "skills" topic (theme 1) on Tuesdays and Thursdays. There is little substantive difference between all this and the student proposal.

As the first option, the staff could offer "language and power" or "sociolinguistics." Staff member 3 suggests starting with "sociolinguistics" and then moving on to "language and power."

Guy: "It's hardly an option if we have no choice."

Laura: "We wanted them to be more informal than you suggest."

Mavis: "And more peripheral, in a way."

Staff member 7 (correcting colleagues): "I thought we decided not to call them options but 'choices'—it needn't be that you do one but not another."

Laura: "What if an individual is fascinated by a topic the way I'm fascinated by affective aspects of learning? I thought we saw the possibility of fitting those things in on Monday afternoons."

There is a general discussion about where such things might be accommodated. Laura notes that the staff have built nothing in so that part-time students can participate in work groups or reading groups.

Staff member 1: "It's always very difficult with part-timers."

Staff member 6: "There's nothing to stop part-timers from doing it on their own."

Laura: "Could part-timers come to the morning sessions?"

Staff member 1: "No problem."

Deirdre: "I enjoyed the Monday lunchtime sessions."

Staff members 4 and 6: "They'll be continued."

Mavis: "But that's mainly for full-time students."

They move on.

Staff member 4: "You've spelt out a particular teaching method that we should follow. We don't think that's fair. We wouldn't prescribe to you how you should teach in your school. The staff are sensitive and will teach in the way they feel best. To order it the way your proposal does is too constraining. I'd like to suggest you just trust us."

Deirdre: "That's very reasonable."

Laura: "But would there be room for us to express a particular interest?"

Staff member 4: "What would you do? Wouldn't you accommodate your students if they expressed a particular interest?" There is some laughter for the first time for two days.

Laura: "Brandon was in a course that wasn't relevant to his situation. He told the instructor and she said, 'Wait; we'll come to it before the end of the year.' He waited until the end of the year, but the relevant part never came."

Staff member 6: "We'll try to do what we can, but we can't set up huge expectations."

Staff member 3: "We do want to address your classroom needs, but you don't know where you'll be in five years' time. I personally found grammar very useful."

Mavis: "It may look as if we don't want to go beyond the classroom, but all our emphasis on theory should indicate the opposite. We've spelt it all out for the first theme just to help you get the picture, but we don't intend to be rigid."

Charles: "What exactly will you cover under 'skills'?"

Staff member 6: "They will include first- and second-language acquisition, which we thought were missing."

Staff member 3: "It has been suggested you need different kinds of grammar for different kinds of purpose—one in relation to language acquisition, for example, and then another in relation to skills. A member of the Linguistics Department is an expert on first-language acquisition who also focuses on grammar systems. That could be taught to you. The instructor could come in to talk with you now if you like."

As students begin to discuss this new possibility among themselves, staff member 3 goes off to get the linguist, who is ready and waiting only a few offices away.

Mavis starts to explain: "Our concern is that we don't get these things in a vacuum, merely academic. We have to see them working for us."

The linguistics instructor enters briskly, takes the seat at the instructor's desk at the front of the group, and gets straight to the point: "I can teach a course on first-language acquisition that leads up to second-language acquisition, which [staff member 1] teaches. We focus on what the two processes have in common, not their differences. We teach various theoretical perspectives—we'd put forward the major theoretical ideas."

Deirdre: "Would you lecture or would it be in seminar form?"

Linguist: "I usually teach like this—to the whole group."

Staff member 1 points to the timetable on the board and explains: "It would fit in under 'alternative language descriptions.'" Staff member 1 adds: "You must consider the value of input. You're clients. We'll respond to your needs. That's what we're paid to do."

The students are busy taking notes.

Guy: "I'd like to know exactly how you're going to meet our needs if there isn't a session for groups. How would you know our implicit theories?"

Staff member 6: "We'd ask you. I mean, I'm going to be teaching reading and writing, I think. I'll ask you what you're interested in."

Guy: "I'd like some clarity on this word 'teach.' Does this mean 'lecture'?"

Gertrude—out of the blue—says: "I don't think I learned much in the past seven weeks, and I had a long drive. I *want* some input."

Staff member 4 picks this up instantly: "Is that the experience of anyone else?"

Guy: "Quite the contrary."

Gertrude: "I think it's different for full-time students." (She is part-time, and Guy is full-time).

Staff member 4, pressing: "Can we go round the room for a response from everyone?"

Guy perseveres with his concerns: "The full-time students wanted to continue the special morning sessions on language learning and teaching for this year's full-time and last year's part-time students. They're also very interested in language and power."

There is a logistical discussion about fitting in these topics for full-time students.

Staff member 6: "We should hear from everyone in the room so that we can start negotiating."

Staff member 4 says: "Some people haven't responded to my question," and starts going round the room, calling on individuals to speak. The students are conciliatory.

Eleanor: "It sounds okay to me."

Faith: "I think everything is being fitted in."

Mavis, going back to Gertrude's comment: "A lot of us, even part-timers, think the past seven weeks have been extremely useful."

Laura: "Absolutely."

Mavis: "We did a lot more thinking."

Staff member 4 is still canvassing opinions about the students' response. Thomas: "Quite accommodating."

Alice: "I don't think we should leave Gertrude out on a limb. I don't fully understand why I had to go through this format. But it was different for us [last-year's part-time students]."

Deirdre: "I think the staff have come a long way to meet us. It's been an interesting process. We learned many things we didn't know at the beginning."

Guy: "This has been one of the more valuable experiences of my life. I shared my ideas with my peers and was valued. I didn't feel at any time disempowered because of a hierarchy. It's the only way to learn."

Gertrude: "I'm happy with the experience I had, but I need to have some input."

Albert: "To me, it has been a very valuable experience, very enlightening. Very nice experience." He adds hopefully: "The new thing looks like what we've been suggesting."

Charles: "I've read things I wouldn't otherwise have read and thought about things I wouldn't otherwise have thought about. It is as difficult for me to understand what you have in mind as it seems to be for you to understand what we have in mind."

Staff member 4 wants to wind up: "I don't think there's anything more to be said. Thank you. We'll see you next session."

Laura: "Did you have time to consider our comments on evaluation?"

Staff member 4: "No. That will take a lot of time."

Laura: "So, what can we anticipate at the end of the next quarter?"

Staff member 4: "We'll come back to that as soon as we can."

Mavis: "We were told the university has lots of flexibility."

Staff member 7 (already moving out of the room): "It's always interesting to examine alternative proposals."

The meeting breaks up quickly for the three-week vacation before second quarter.

Chapter 17

Aftermath

A t Codesa, the ANC made new proposals for power sharing during the transition to a more representative and democratic form of government. A spokesman for the government immediately dismissed the ANC proposals as "ludicrous" and "insulting."

I BEGAN MY PREPARATIONS to leave the course, the university, and the country. Had I stayed, I would have had to participate in preplanned instruction, assignments, marking, and grading—and I could not in conscience do this with the students I had worked with.

I chaired a final, brief departmental meeting at which the Honours course was not mentioned except for a further discussion of who might teach particular topics. Later, I was unofficially asked to conduct a small seminar for a few members of the academic staff who wanted to explore matters of language and learning, especially reading and writing. Some of the Honours students also called in to ask if I would run an informal seminar for them before I left and to invite me to a party.

One of my colleagues told me the "real reason" they had become alienated was that they had been denied access to the student deliberations. They had thought the meetings would be a staff-student collaboration and had become very anxious and hurt when shut out after a few sessions, even though the exclusion had been a decision of the students. They thought they had a right and a need to observe what was going on.

Explanation that the collaboration would have begun after the students had had sufficient opportunity to work out an independent position did not satisfy them. They wanted to be *there*. The fact that students could contact the staff as often as they wished—which many of them did—also did not satisfy them. They felt "betrayed" by being excluded.

As a farewell token, one of my colleagues gave me a small stone tortoise.

170

I SEE NO POINT IN DRAWING CONCLUSIONS and providing recommendations, merely for the sake of doing so. The participants in the seminar thought for themselves, relating the considerations of this book to their own attitudes and circumstances, and readers will do the same. The opinions of the seventeen students are clear enough, without the need for signposts or summary from me, and there are obviously no quick and easy "solutions." The underlying problems in education in South Africa, as in so many other places, are essentially political, not educational, and the only resolution must be political, at many levels.

It seems even clearer to me now that authority determines the roles that language plays. Rather than empowering students, the English-language requirements imposed on black students in the school and university settings described in this book held students back, interfering with their intellectual and academic development. Language was a weapon used against them, even if unintentionally—a weapon not available to them in return because they did not have the power to say how language should be employed.

AN HONOURS STUDENT COMMENTED that the members of the group had not been good at visiting one another's schools. They had not known what to look for, and they tended to see what was going on from the point of view of teacher behaviour, not student response.

The course experience had been a surprise for all of them. They were not prepared for it. Some thought it great; others did not. It had been particularly difficult for students who had been out of the academic world for several years. Their personal resources were limited. They would sometimes have appreciated more guidance but recognized that I was on a tightrope. Some students also thought they would have benefited from closer collaboration with staff, who could have helped them to interpret their experience—but this was another tightrope.

The greatest outcome had been the bonding that took place among the students, who learned about each other. They doubted if it would have taken place in any other way among such a varied group.

Some also thought my leaving was a cop-out.

FOR GUY, IT WAS THE END OF THE *JOL*. To the dismay of other members of the group, he decided to discontinue his studies immediately. Less dramatically, Benjamin dropped out before the mid-year examinations. Charles and Mavis, who were both eligible to move out of the Honours course into the master's programme, elected to do so. The master's degree in the department is "untaught," with a supervised dissertation requirement but no lectures or examinations.

The other Honours students, I have been told, remained a close-knit group as they returned to the usual Wits routine. There was a "wonderfully unpre-scriptive" skills course with two staff members who allowed students to follow their own interests. But the students also received the conventional lectures on syntax, sociolinguistics, and testing. They had little time to spend together because of "pressure of work," especially cramming for the examinations.

THE TOWNSHIP VIOLENCE CONTINUED under the eyes of the rest of the world. A human rights commission reported that over 13,000 black people had died in township violence since 1984—nearly half of them in the two years since the official end of apartheid. Reports of systematic police torture of black prisoners were confirmed by the white doctor who had performed autopsies on hundreds of the mutilated bodies. He said he could no longer keep silent.

In the wake of further massacres, the Codesa talks collapsed. There was a two-day general strike of black workers, followed by a demonstration outside Parliament in Pretoria calling for an end to violence, the vote for all South Africans, and a transitional government. Nelson Mandela also appealed for the United Nations to intervene, and for the first time, an outside special rep-resentative and a team of observers were sent to South Africa.

An "integrated" group of South African athletes participated in the Olympic Games in Barcelona, though not under the South African flag. The world's television cameras focused prominently on Mandela in the stands—as if he were already the official representative of South Africa. He was gaining international authority and recognition, though few people saw anything he had written in English or in any other language.

References

Brown, R. G. (1991). *Schools of thought: How the politics of literacy shape thinking in the classroom.* San Francisco: Jossey-Bass.

Brumfit, C. (1984). The Bangalore procedural syllabus. *ELT Journal, 38,* 233–241.

Canale, M., & Swain, M. (1980). Theoretical bases of communicative approaches to second language teaching and testing. *Applied Linguistics, 1,* 1–47.

Cummins, J., & Swain, M. (1986). *Bilingualism in education: Aspects of theory, research and practice.* New York: Longman.

de Villiers, M. (1987). *White tribe dreaming: Apartheid's bitter roots.* Toronto: Macmillan.

Elley, W. B. (1991). Acquiring literacy in a second language: The effect of book-based programs. *Language Learning, 41,* 375–411.

Harlech-Jones, B. (1991). *You taught me language.* Cape Town: Oxford University Press.

Hartshorne, K. B. (1987). Language policy in African education in South Africa 1910–1985 with particular reference to the issue of medium of instruction. In D. Young (Ed.), *Language: Planning and medium in education* (pp. 82–106). Rondebosh, South Africa: University of Cape Town Language Education Unit and Southern African Applied Linguistics Association.

Janks, H. (1990). Contested terrain: English education in South Africa 1948–1987. In I. Goodson & P. Medway (Eds.), *Bringing English to order* (pp. 242–261). Philadelphia: Falmer Press.

Kallaway, P. (Ed.). (1984). *Apartheid and education: The education of black South Africans.* Johannesburg: Raven.

Kane-Berman, J. (1978). *Soweto: Black revolt, white reaction.* Johannesburg: Raven.

Krashen, S. (1985). *Inquiries and insights.* Menlo Park, CA: Alemany Press.

Krashen, S. (1991a). Bilingual education: A focus on current research. *Focus, 3.*

Krashen, S. (1991b). Sheltered subject matter teaching. *Cross Currents, 18,* 183–188.

Macdonald, C., & Burroughs, E. (1991). *Eager to talk and learn and think: Bilingual primary education in South Africa.* Cape Town: Maskew Miller Longman.

Malan, R. (1990). *My traitor's heart.* New York: Vintage International.

McLean, D. (1991). Language policy in a new South Africa: A mild form of oppression? *Rhodes Review,* 17–18.

Moll, L. C. (Ed.). (1990). *Vygotsky and education: Instrumental implications and applications of socio-historical psychology.* Cambridge: Cambridge University Press.

Murray, S. (1991). Developing language competencies of the student teacher. *ELTIC Reporter, 16,* 3–10.

Paulston, C. B. (1987). Linguistic consequences of ethnicity and nationalism in multilingual settings. In D. Young (Ed.), *Language: Planning and medium in edu-*

cation (pp. 12–57). Rondebosh, South Africa: University of Cape Town Language Education Unit and Southern African Applied Linguistics Association.

Prabhu, N. S. (1987). *Second language pedagogy.* Oxford: Oxford University Press.

Sacks, O. (1989). *Seeing voices.* Berkeley, CA: University of California Press.

Schadeberg, J. (Ed.). (1990). *Nelson Mandela and the rise of the ANC.* Parklands, South Africa: Ball and Donker.

Smith, F. (1986). *Insult to intelligence.* Portsmouth, NH: Heinemann.

Smith, F. (1987). *Joining the literacy club.* Portsmouth, NH: Heinemann Educational Books.

Smith, F. (1989). Overselling literacy. *Phi Delta Kappan, 7*(5), 352–359.

Smith, F. (1990). *To think.* New York: Teachers College Press.

Vygotsky, L. S. (1978). *Mind in society.* Cambridge, MA: Harvard University Press.

Vygotsky, L. S. (1987). Thinking and speech. In L. S. Vygotsky, *Collected works.* New York: Plenum.

Webb, C. M. (1986). *Teacher education and training: Colleges of education.* Paper presented at the Human Resources Research Council Conference on the Role of Black Education, Pretoria, South Africa.

Willinsky, J. (1984). *The well-tempered tongue: The politics of standard English in the classroom.* New York: Lang.

Young, D. (Ed.). (1987). *Language: Planning and medium in education.* Rondebosh, South Africa: University of Cape Town Language Education Unit and Southern African Applied Linguistics Association.

About the Author

FRANK SMITH was born in London, England. He took his undergraduate degree at the University of Western Australia and has a Ph.D. from Harvard University.

He was a reporter and editor on the staff of a number of newspapers and magazines in Europe and Australia and has been a researcher on many projects concerned with literacy and language education. He was a professor at the Universities of Toronto and Victoria for fifteen years and was visiting professor and head of the new Department of Applied English Language Studies at the University of the Witwatersrand in Johannesburg, South Africa, during the events recounted in this book.

Frank Smith has published short stories, poetry, a novel, and sixteen books concerned with language and education. He lives on Vancouver Island in British Columbia, Canada.